An Unlikely Gift

Lauren Boswell Blair

WestBow Press
A Division of Thomas Nelson

WestBow Press books may be ordered through booksellers or by contacting:

WestBow Press
A Division of Thomas Nelson
1663 Liberty Drive
Bloomington, IN 47403
www.westbowpress.com
1 (866) 928-1240

ISBN: 978-1-4908-1481-0 (sc)
ISBN: 978-1-4908-1482-7 (e)

Library of Congress Control Number: 2013920405

Printed in the United States of America.

WestBow Press rev. date: 11/27/2013

All royalties will be donated to Kupenda
for the Children: www.kupenda.org.
Thank you for your contribution!

To my husband, Patrick, for introducing me to a cause and lifestyle that is larger than the two of us; to my parents for believing I could author a book ever since I learned how to write; and to my sister, Sarah, for reminding me of this when I needed it most.

Nakupenda

CONTENTS

PREFACE

This book was birthed out of a desire to shed light on the plight of one of the most underprivileged groups that exist in the world today, children with disabilities. Not only does this population embody the vulnerability unique to children, but they endure bodies that are not always able to outwardly reflect the potential within. Perhaps most limiting of all, however, are the barriers that communities place on this population's worth and potential. When I think of the people Christ kept in his company, it is hard for me to imagine a community that would bring him more joy than the children with disabilities in Kenya.

I have done my best to align what, due to human error, amounts to slightly varying accounts of events by different sources. All biblical references are taken from the New International Version of the Bible. Whenever possible, I have tried to use disability-appropriate language, although what is preferred language in the United States may not be the same as the preferred language in Kenya. I apologize and take full responsibility for any inaccurate or potentially offensive language.

I urge the reader to recognize that the focus on the gaping need of services to children with disabilities in Kenya is not analogous to Kenya's development as a whole. Historically, Kenya has been and remains one of the greatest success stories in Africa post-emancipation. During my own visits, I have been humbled by the way I have been taken in by various communities and how they have dealt so graciously and patiently with my blunders. It is a learning process to understand a foreign culture on both sides of the equation, and, admittedly, I have a long way to go before becoming "proficient." Consequently, I ask the reader not to interpret my words as condemning or patronizing but as a call to arms in regard to a humanitarian condition that is best alleviated in partnership together.

I have also removed myself from the story almost entirely to avoid any perception of personal gain. Additionally, all book profits will be donated to Kupenda for the Children (www.kupenda.org), an organization that assists children with disabilities in Kenya. I have considered it an honor to participate behind the scenes in the work being done for children with disabilities. In 2007, when I first volunteered with Kupenda in Kenya, the founder, Cynthia Bauer, was almost hesitant to allow me to come along. Historically, my health, history of pediatric surgeries, and slight build make me, at first glance, not appear to be the most suitable candidate for the rigors of volunteer work on the ground in Kenya. Thankfully though, God finds amusement in raising up the most unlikely of candidates for his work. Due to a geographic detail, I was offered medical assistance that prevented the onset of a disability, which is unlikely the case if I had lived in Kenya. From my first visit until the present, Kupenda has grown to be an integral part of my life and my marriage. My husband, Patrick Blair, is also heavily invested. He cofounded and directs one of Kupenda's largest support organizations, Adventures for the Cure (www.adventuresforthecure.com) with his friend Adam Driscoll. Meanwhile, I have proudly been acting as chairperson of Kupenda's board of directors, a role that allows me to confidently attest to the authenticity of the stories that follow.

Throughout the book-writing process, I have been indebted to Leonard Mbonani, who spent hours arranging interviews and hosting me in the generous manner typical of the people of Kenya. The achievements made in this book in the mission to assist children with disabilities have largely occurred because we stand on the shoulders of his efforts and expertise.

Additionally, I am particularly grateful to Cynthia Bauer for helping get this project started and for entrusting me with the very personal details of her life. Over the past six years I have personally witnessed the extent of Cindy's daily sacrifices to love these children who often slip by unnoticed. I can attest to how quickly she will give up her own personal comfort, whether going years without receiving a salary or at times even going without heat in her home to serve her mission. I've also benefited from her ability to share in the difficult places of a loved one's life. Just like the very word *compassion*, which means "to suffer with," Cindy goes beyond mere sentiments and gets her hands dirty loving others. Over the course of the three years I spent writing this book, I endured numerous miscarriages and a failed adoption. In the midst of this, she waited patiently for me to write when I was able to write. She also got in the trenches and grieved with me.

These things make me that much more grateful for the meaning of this story and what God is ultimately able to bring out of brokenness. I only hope that I have imparted even a fraction of its full value in the chapters that follow.

Cindy and Leonard, what I have written, you have lived. The stories you shared with me were life-changing, the mission you allowed me to take part in a privilege. May we follow your example and learn to see value in what was once considered an unlikely place.

Lauren Boswell Blair

The author, Lauren Boswell Blair, with students at the Gede Special School in 2010.

ACKNOWLEDGEMENTS

The author would like to acknowledge the Lord, who created this story in the first place and who gave me the strength to finish writing it; the children of Kupenda who are no longer with us but are never forgotten; my husband, for lovingly supporting me throughout this book process, for listening to every chapter read out loud, and for providing feedback in a way that only he can get away with; my sister, Sarah Boswell, for helping design the cover through Styled by Seb (www.zazzle.com/StyledbySeb); and Julie-Ann Burkhart for designing the banner graphics. Additional thanks to Jessica Alston of Jessica Alston Photography (www.jessicalalstonphotorgraphy.com) for the author photo; Brian McLaren for tutoring me on how to run a board of directors, for his insight into the book world, for his time taken to provide manuscript feedback, and for his relentless efforts to connect me with the right people. You have an uncanny ability to make people feel important by creating time and space for them when there is none; others who provided editing and insight into the manuscript, including Leonard Mbonani, Cynthia Bauer, and Jeff Gentry. Particular thanks go to Alyssa Ranney Walker for her initial appraisal of the book proposal and editing sample chapters. Thanks also to Ben Rhodes at the Christian Institute on Disability for proofreading for disability-appropriate language. Additional thanks to Ken Zeigler at Wellspring Counseling (www.wellspringlifecounseling.com) for his character profile of Cynthia Bauer; those who allowed me to conduct interviews with them in both the United States and Kenya, including Koffa Edwin Abio, Alanna Ahlers, Rashid Athman, Andrew Bauer, Cynthia Bauer, Dick Bauer, Kate Bauer, Sandra Bauer, Scott Belfit, Patrick Blair, Dr. Dick Bransford, Brian Buell, Jacob and Julie-Ann Burkhart, Laura Claiborne, Rebecca Cross, Adam Driscoll, Maryline Faida, Melissa Kane, Martha Karo, Thomas Katana,

Anthony Jomo Kenyatta Jr., Chengo Kithi, Pastor Ken Lawrence, Nhu Lee, Rev. Robert Mangi, Anthony Maranto, Zurhura Masemo, Leonard Mbonani, Janet Mbonani, Fran McConnell, George Charo Mweri, Gabriel Mwnengo, Victoria Ndaa, Willy Nganda, Beatrice Plowman, Patricia Prasada-Rao, Brianna Riddell, Julie Rowland, Assistant Chief Sirya, Ken Turmet, Thelitha Wachu, Randy Wilbur, Virginia Wilbur, Dr. Dick Wright, Teresia Zawadi, and Elizabeth Nthenya Mutie. Additional thanks to the family members of Janet Mbonani, Winnie Gona, Oliver Ngala, Charo Shida, and Joyce Wanje; Emily Boop for documenting Kenyan laws and policies regarding disabilities; the Kupenda for the Children board of directors and advisory board: Andrew Bauer, Cynthia Bauer, Sandra Bauer, Patrick Blair, Jeff Gentry, Anthony Maranto, Carissa Mortenson, Patricia Prasada-Rao, and Rev. Randy Wilbur; the Kuhenza for the Children staff and board of directors: Cynthia Bauer, Elinah Bendera, Norbert Deche, Maryline Faida, Joseph Gona, Martha Karo, Oripa Zuma Kweke, Rev. Robert Mangi, Leonard Mbonani, Silas Mutwiri Migwi, Margaret Mwiti, Gabriel Mwnengo, and Gertrude Mwenda William; Adventures for the Cure and many other Kupenda supporters who have helped carry this mission and continue to make it possible; and, as always, Cynthia Bauer, friend and co-conspirator.

CHAPTER 1

THE STRENGTH OF STIGMA

My frame was not hidden from you when I was made in the secret place, when I was woven together in the depths of the earth.—Psalm 139:15

Kenya, 1978

Even the earth contracted in labored lines of thirst. Just a few feet away lay Kache, her muscles tightening and shortening, laboring against the tiny body inside her. Balancing on the precipice of a stool, Kache squatted with the support of a piece of lace, horseshoed around her waist and harnessed by the midwife in front of her. Another midwife buttressed the mother's shoulders from behind while yet another crouched in anticipation of the slick newborn's body. At fifty-five, this was Kache's twenty-first child.

Her husband was away tending to the *shamba*, the desperately infertile tract of land in which he toiled to grow corn. They lived hand to mouth in a migratory settlement, shifting with the crops and livestock in the rural bush area of Ramada, Kenya. Today the sun hung round and bulbous. The ground underneath it was dry, red, and unforgiving. The bush in the dusty soil lay sparsely scattered about like a multitude of thorny, brown tentacles. In the distance a spotty perimeter of trees clung to sustenance along the banks of the sediment-filled lake. The alvera tree her husband planted stood firmly rooted to the northeast of the *mdzi*, the homestead where Kache labored. The thatched roof sheltered the women as they gathered between the four walls of her mud hut made of dried earth insulating a scaffolding of tethered twigs.

Two of the women assisting Kache were midwives from the village, but also in attendance was another of her husband's wives. Kache rescued her as a six-year-old from being sold into marriage by an uncle greedy for a profit. Allowing the girl to marry her own husband, Kache watched over her until she was old enough to take on the duties of a wife. Today her husband had four wives, but it was Kache who held the esteemed position of elder wife and successful child bearer. She was a vigorous woman, resilient in physical endurance and resolved in her tenacity to govern the actions of her family. While her husband was the head of the household in title, she embodied the matriarchal role with dictatorial firmness.

She continued her labor, tightening her grip on the sides of the stool. The tawny skin along her hands pulled tautly across her knuckles. Her head bent toward her chest, her closely cropped hair beading in perspiration at its roots. She exhaled deeply, resolving for this delivery to be her last.

The previous nine months of carrying this child had been relatively peaceful. The baby did not even disturb her with a gentle nudge or a playful kick. Over the past twenty-one hours of labor, however, she wove a tapestry of colorful condemnations and guttural groans. Even the midwives whispered concern. The closest hospital was in Malindi, a journey more than twenty miles away. The women considered carrying her on a traditional tribal bed with wood frame and knotted rope, but in her obstinacy, she refused to move from the cluster of huts she called home.

It was now the second sunrise of her labor. Digging in her heels, she summoned every fiber and sinew. When her contractions reached their apogee, the child slowly began to emerge from the security of her womb. Then Kache cried out. The legs of the infant preceded the head in a painful breech. Her jaw clenched in paroxysms of pain.

Concealed in a nearby hut, her fifteen-year-old daughter, Janet, listened to the cries of her mother with rapt interest. Her brother's purple body was thrust forward into the world, clubbed feet first, which emerged at a 180-degree angle with his toes pointing behind him. In another second, the infant contorted and its head materialized, his aberrant wail issuing forth as a loud, catlike roar, alarming everyone within hearing distance.

"*Mvulana*," she murmured, "a boy."

The midwife reached up and unwrapped her *kanga*, the traditional cloth wound and knotted around her head. Using the corner, she began to swab away the amniotic fluid. It was then that she recognized another irregularity: a deep depression lay where the boy's nose and mouth should connect, a condition known as a cleft palate.

Kache, defeated by twenty-one hours of childbirth, cried out in exhaustion. "I was dying, and now I have given birth to such a child!"

She questioned how to care for a child unable to drink from her breast and how to endure the scorn of the community that considered a disability to be a curse from God. "This is not a child to care for," she admitted. After a long silence, she instructed the midwives.

From her seat nearby, Janet heard the midwives exit the hut and hasten down the path. Along with them she heard the piercing cry of her brother asserting his will to live.

When they came to the white trunk of the mkone tree just a short distance from the lake, one of the wives stood by and watched. As a family member and Kache's designated representative, she was bound by tradition to act as a witness.

The women laid the infant on the ground, its protective cloth inadvertently slipping open. The baby's eyes squeezed shut and his fingers gripped into fists, curling tightly to bring back the security of his mother's womb.

The midwife laid the baby into a shallow depression dug into the dirt that was soon filled with water.

Inside the ground, the infant's cries continued.

The midwives offered the child's "curse" to the mkone tree in hopes of future blessings.

Yet inside the ground, the infant's cries continued.

As the women filled the depression with dirt, the earth became level—as if barely ever disturbed.

But inside the infant lay still beneath their feet.

CHAPTER 2

AN UNLIKELY GIFT

But he said to me, "My grace is sufficient for you, for my power is made perfect in weakness."—2 Corinthians 12:9

New York, March 7, 1974

Four years earlier in the United States, another infant lay in Sandra's arms. The fluorescent hospital lighting created a starchy halo around the bustle of nurses checking on every breath and pulse. When the clamor died down a nurse handed her a note, hoping to bring her comfort in spite of the palpable grief surrounding her.

It was the summer of 1973. Dick, twenty-two, and Sandra, twenty-four, were married for one year when they moved into their two-bedroom apartment in Rochester, New York. Dick was offered a promising engineering job with the Eastman Kodak Company while Sandra discovered she was pregnant just a few days before the move. The news was elating but left her apprehensive. With five dollars a week, she prepared the nursery for the new arrival and reordered their lives, box by box, detail by detail.

By the time March rolled around, the doctor informed her that things were progressing normally. To Sandra, delivery was still a distant prospect and nothing to be alarmed about. When her water broke shortly afterward, she remained calm. In her mind there was plenty of time. To Dick, that meant an extra couple of hours to hit some balls around before leaving for the hospital. At taller than six feet, Dick had the muscular body of a natural athlete. An avid baseball fan, the unseasonably warm seventy-degree weather taunted him with the possibility of unwinding before the long hours ahead.

When evening arrived, the pair headed to Northside Hospital, where the doctor confirmed that she was in labor. Once the nurses wheeled her into her room, however, the fevered screams of the woman in the next bed began to unsettle her.

After seven hours of contractions, she tried to lift herself off the bed to use the bathroom. As she swung her legs over the side, a nurse rushed over to push her back while calling for an operating room over her shoulder. As the baby began to emerge, Dick was ushered aside and Sandra began to experience the chemical warmth of the anesthesia lulling her into its sleepy embrace.

New York, March 8, 1974

When Sandra finally woke, it was to a sea of concerned faces that caused her to fear whether her baby was even alive. The doctor approached her bedside and explained the details of the baby's condition. Desperate to see her new little girl, Sandra was told to wait.

After the hours painfully ticked by, a nurse took pity on her and stealthily slipped the child into Sandra's room. The seven pound, bulbous-bellied infant was swaddled in the hospital blanket, sleepily scrunched into its warmth like a cocoon. Sandra held her close. She felt her heart expanding at just the sight of her. This was her beautiful baby girl, Cynthia Rose. She had wisps of the brunette-colored hair of both her parents. Together the couple identified their features in her petite face.

With a swell of apprehension, she unwrapped the blanket and let her finger be entwined by Cynthia's right fist. When she looked at Cynthia's left arm, she noticed that it stopped short a few inches below her elbow. Instead, the arm rounded off with tiny fingertips protruding from its end. As she would learn later, the congenital limb deficiency most likely occurred between the fourth and eighth weeks of gestation. The bud of her arm had failed to send correct messages to other cells during limb formation. As a result, there was a vacuous space where her bones would have formed a bridge from her elbow to her wrist. For the time being, however, Sandra was still uncertain what caused her daughter's condition.

She experienced a range of emotions—elation that her baby was alive, but concern about her daughter's future. Suddenly she was questioning all the details of her pregnancy that could have affected her child. Even the X-rays taken without a lead vest at the dentist's office were now suspects. Although usually prone to anxiety, Sandra eventually surrendered to a peaceful voice inside her that said God was in control. As a child, she had encountered a powerful missionary from Haiti who was mostly blind. If God could establish power through this man, he could do the same for Cynthia. She knew it with absolute certainty.

After the nurse covertly returned the infant to the nursery, Sandra read over the note she was given. Inside was a poem titled "Children Learn What They Live," by Dorothy Law Nolte, PhD. One of the lines stated, "If children live with acceptance, they learn to love." The poem continued to emphasize that the way in which children are treated is the way they will go on to view themselves and in turn treat others. She pondered the comforting words of reassurance and let them have weight in her mind. She realized that protecting Cynthia would only teach her to be ashamed. She resolved to love her child in a way that empowered her to live beyond the body that encased her.

Next to Sandy, Dick struggled for composure. His mind became an avalanche of concerns, gaining momentum as he fast forwarded the difficulties of his child's future in his mind. In his grief, he wracked his brain to determine what he might do for his daughter. Convinced that God would be glorified through the restoration of his daughter's arm, he determined to fast. He decided not to let another piece of food touch his lips until Cynthia's hand was healed.

CHAPTER 3

THE WORK OF YOUR HAND

A man's deeds are of greater importance than the facts of his birth.—African Proverb

Kenya, 1986

Leonard asked for her hand. Eight years after her brother's birth and murder, Janet stood before the Ramada schoolteacher and family friend struggling to respond to his proposal for marriage. Under the shade of the coral block school building, her angry tears began an avalanche of sleek pathways over her prominent cheekbones. Leonard detected the haughty energy underneath the proud eyes he admired.

When he questioned her distress at length, she gestured with her hand, her response resolute. "Just go," she responded. "Just go home."

Kenya, 1965

Nestled in the brush of Arabuko, eight-year-old Leonard, who had recently migrated with his parents from Kakuyuni, watched his aunt Dzingo desperately trying to communicate with his family. The others taunted her hand movements with amusement.

"Look at this woman!" they exclaimed. "She does not even know how to speak!"

Aunt Dzingo turned her back to them, bearing their animosity with a quiet rage. Stooping, she continued toiling with the farm work. The work of her hands was like a sieve. Only a fraction of what she produced from the land was kept for herself. Only a fraction of what she tried to convey was understood.

Just a short distance away, Leonard witnessed the suffering of his aunt with compassion. He knew that aunt Dzingo was not a difficult woman. Aunt Dzingo was deaf. Rather than appreciating what she produced, the others detected her vulnerability and translated it into a weakness to be avoided.

In the family's current state of affairs, each day ended with uncertainty. Previously they had survived off of the wages his father earned in the illegal ivory trade. Unfortunately, many years ago, his father had disappeared under the blanket of night to transport a full lorry of ivory to the heavily populated port city of Mombasa. During the journey, the police intercepted him and sentenced him to three long years in jail. Within a short time, the harsh conditions of prison life deteriorated his strength. By the time he was released, he was anemic. Although his brothers took him to an herbalist for treatment, the condition worsened. After taking him to the Malindi District Hospital, he ultimately passed away.

Without his provision, Leonard's family depended entirely on what they tilled from the land. In accordance with the culture, his mother remarried her husband's younger brother, and Leonard was joined by eight other children he considered siblings, although over time, only two of them would survive the harsh conditions. Even Leonard's uncle became afflicted with leprosy. This put even more pressure on his mother, Jumwa Nzai, who had to labor extensively to support her boys. In fact, to the community, she became known as *hawazazawidi jumwa jembe*, or "the woman who depends entirely on the hoe." In Kenya, a combination of manual labor, malnutrition, and inadequate care often contributed to the low life expectancy of forty-five years. Each day she worked on the farm, Leonard assisting her until he left for class where the school committee had graciously exempted him from paying school fees.

When Leonard entered secondary school about twelve miles away, he depended on the charity of a bursary fund run by an area member of parliament to pay for his room and board. He also held odd jobs to help make ends meet. His wages came from construction, cutting trees, or catching fish. At the nearby Mida Creek, he used a special technique to increase his catch. He placed poisonous bark from a local tree into the water, causing the fish to float to the surface. Fortunately, the substance was not toxic for humans. On days where even this strategy failed him, he was left hungry and exhausted.

Through all his efforts, Leonard managed to sustain himself and perform exceedingly well in his studies. In 1980, while he waited to attend college, he decided to take employment with the government as an untrained teacher. At the end of the month, he enthusiastically received his first paycheck of eight dollars. With the money in his pocket he journeyed home, intercepting his mother as she looked for work. When he articulated that she no longer needed to labor for other people, he broke down and wept. Hawazawidi Jumwa Jembe was finally given permission to live without fighting, to love without providing, and to relish what she had coveted—the savory vindication of rest.

By 1981, Leonard continued to establish himself. He was admitted to the Primary Teacher's College for two years of courses in teacher training. After watching people bully his aunt, he aspired to teach the deaf and stop the dehumanizing treatment of others. When he concluded his studies, he applied for a teaching position to gain experience before advancing to special-needs training. After he submitted his application, he waited with eager anticipation for his first post. By the time he received the letter from the Ministry of Education in 1983, his excitement transformed to despair. His first post was at a primary school in Ramada, one of the most remote areas to be posted. He felt as if someone had sentenced him to a desert island.

With a heavy heart, he reported to Ramada, where he was disarmed after encountering the extent of the people's kindness. In fact, two brothers who were his students often invited him to their home for meals. It was on one such visit that they introduced him to their sister, Janet, who was home on school break. Although he did not have many opportunities to talk with her, his path eventually coincided with hers again when he got on board a local *matatu*. The public van was filled with passengers, its exterior covered in a patina of dirt. Today, instead of the loud blare of the radio, the passengers began creating their own music. Singing together,

Leonard couldn't help but notice that when Janet joined in, her voice superseded them all.

As his interest piqued, Leonard signed up to manage a plot of land owned by Janet's family. Endeavoring to get to know her better, he was stupefied when the headstrong girl wasn't easily accessible. At twenty-three, Janet was still finishing her studies after being admitted to school at the late age of fourteen. Her family had delayed sending her after her sister was abused and impregnated by the headmaster. While her mother, Kache, had tried to protect her from the same fate, the village leadership threatened to take action if she did not send her children to school.

On the Saturday morning that Leonard asked for her hand in marriage, Janet thought of many things. She thought of her education. She thought of the men in her village who took a wife like they were purchasing property, accumulating more and more. She also thought of her mother's words: "When you get married, you will die."

Although Leonard was a friend, she was inexorable in her refusal. She did not want marriage to prevent her from making something of herself. Out of respect, she did not tell anyone about their meeting. She knew that if her mother discovered his plans, she would surely intervene and drive him off the farm.

As the week slid by, Janet did everything in her power to avoid talking to or even seeing him. For almost two years, her elusive behavior allowed her to think she had succeeded.

CHAPTER 4

IRON PANTS

Do not let what you cannot do tear from your hands what you can.—African Proverb

New York, March 22, 1974

Back at home, Cynthia's father, Dick, struggled with his daughter's disability. Although he eventually resumed eating, he still struggled to understand God's intentions and exactly how he was supposed to respond. As a new Christian and an engineer, he was uncomfortable with such mysterious gray areas. Thankfully, Sandra's parents, Gerard and Virginia Wilbur, agreed to meet with Dick where they listened to him string together his list of anxieties, dwelling on each one with fervor like a bead in a rosary. He struggled with the future limitations his daughter might experience and how others might view her. Amid all his worries, his family surrounded him with affirmation. Gerard insisted, "You just watch … God is going to use her."

Dick's father, Dick senior, also wrote a letter: "I'm still convinced that Cindy will cause a miracle in all of our families. I know that she has caused changes in me. I'm sure that all of us became better acquainted as a result of her birth. So I can see nothing but good things happening. There is no doubt in my mind that she is going to be someone very special in all her life."

Cynthia Bauer with her parents, Dick and Sandra, in 1974.

The next couple of years were not without their trials and tribulations. At Strong Memorial Hospital, Cindy's doctors debated the benefits of a prosthetic. According to the orthopedic surgeon, Cindy needed to wear an artificial arm to prevent damage to her vision from doing too many things in close proximity. The pediatrician, however, expressed concern over the potentially permanent nerve damage that might be caused by a prosthetic. Due to the length of Cindy's arm, it was difficult for the prosthetic to grab hold of the tip in a way that did not squeeze uncomfortably tight and limit sensation. The prosthetic was weighty and cumbersome, even hindering Cindy's ability to crawl. Indicative of her future willfulness, Cindy would fling it aside as she inched across the floor. Eventually, Sandra and Dick put Cindy in a play station on wheels to develop her leg muscles. In just a short time, the active toddler bypassed her crawling stage and continued straight to walking.

Despite his anxiety, Dick showered her with love. He was the first to express affection with a warm hug and to sit and read to her each evening.

In a couple of years, Cindy was joined by her younger sister, Minna. When the expanding family visited Sandra's parents in Maine, the grandparents often spent long hours doting on their grandchildren. Cindy's grandfather, in particular, spent extra time with her, encouraging and affirming her abilities. One afternoon, as the family was cleaning up after lunch, Gerard asked Cindy to put her leftover soda in the fridge.

Cindy looked up at her grandfather, the brown wisps of hair spilling out of her ponytail and into her pouty face. "But I've only got one hand, Grampy."

Gerard's response was resolute. "Cindy," he said, "that one hand took it out and that one hand will put it back!"

With a mischievous smile, Cindy returned the bottle. Like most children, she continued to test her limits, but her family refused to encourage an attitude of limitation. Gerard often quoted from Proverbs, "Start children off in the way they should go, and even when they are old they will not turn from it."

By the time Cindy was ready for preschool, her parents ignored advice about putting Cindy in a special-needs program and enrolled her in "Fit by Five," a nursery school that, more so than others, particularly focused on physical fitness.

Despite the teachers' concerns, Sandra's response was firm. "Don't worry about showing her," she said. "You do what you do, and she'll make her own adaptations."

By 1979 Sandra and Dick decided to relocate to be closer to Sandra's family. Dick found a position with Eastman Kodak in Peabody, Massachusetts, and the family packed up their things and moved to a suburb in Hampton, New Hampshire. Within a year of their arrival, Cindy's little brother, Andrew, joined the Bauer clan. The proximity of their grandparents offered support for the growing family and provided yet another source of steady encouragement for little Cindy. Her grandfather, in particular, looked upon Cindy with favoritism. He envisioned a bright future for Cindy. In Gerard's mind, the only thing that could hold his granddaughter back was her own self-perception.

A devout minister and former soldier, Gerard was a natural leader. He embodied an ambitious will and the magnetism to draw out the accomplishments of others. When he joined the army in 1943, he deftly took on the duties of a flight maintenance engineer and a turret gunner on a B-17. His plane, similar to his demeanor, was affectionately known as

"Iron Pants." It was during one of his flights that his plane crash landed in France where he was shot at and eventually captured by the Germans. Over the next year the other prisoners learned to depend on Gerard's wilderness skills from his upbringing in Maine. When times were difficult, he was known to skin a wandering cat to supplement their meager rations.

Yet another life-changing aspect of his imprisonment was when a pastor visited him and told him God had saved him for a purpose. The thought became a buoy for him and, after his release, compelled him to earn a plethora of degrees in business, the Bible, education, and counseling. His new credentials helped him have a profound impact on the students he taught and the congregation he pastored.

When he looked at Cindy, he saw the same limitless potential. Her long afternoons with him were full of teaching and adventure. One August when Cindy was eight years old, they decided to harvest blueberries near their home. When the novelty of being in the blueberry field wore off and was replaced with tedium, Cindy persisted in filling her pail. When it was time to carry her weighty harvest to the winnowing machine to separate the field debris from the fruit, she defiantly turned down offers for help. She responded with consternation, "I can carry my own, and I can winnow my own!"

Amused by Cindy's inherent determination, Gerard spent hours with her traipsing through the woods nearby, teaching her about porcupine needles and spruce gum, and canoeing through the glittering water of Webb Pond.

Although Cindy never failed to accomplish all that was set before her, it was not long before she discovered the challenge of convincing others. When her sister, Minna, expressed an interest in the piano, she excitedly joined in. When they approached Sandra, she reflected on it, knowing the difficulty of learning to play with one arm. She set to work teaching her daughters the basics, and over time, the girls received lessons from a local instructor. As the girls practiced, Cindy tried to adapt by using the tip of her left arm as a sixth finger while the instructor's deaf cat, erroneously named Mozart, snoozed heartily nearby. When the girls were ready to progress to the next level, Sandra went on to consult the organist at church, who welcomed Minna as a student but was at a loss for how to develop Cindy's ability to technical proficiency. As a result, Cindy resorted to teaching herself.

Yet another time while on a bike ride, her companion enthusiastically told everyone, "Cindy was so fast—even with one arm!"

As Cindy discovered, it was not uncommon for people to confuse one disability with another, as if having one arm affected her legs.

Occasionally at school, Cindy also experienced the pangs of being different among her peers. Her prosthesis, in the shape of a hook, dubbed her the deplorable nickname "Captain Hook." Such monikers made her hide her arm protectively in her pocket and caused her to dread meeting new people and loathe having to talk about her condition.

Whenever Cindy received a new prosthetic, her mother gathered the neighborhood children around to demonstrate it, hoping to quell their curiosity once and for all. To Cindy, the novelty was what she lived with daily. It was no longer new or interesting and she refused to be deterred from her ambitions. When she wanted to play softball, she modeled herself after Jim Abbott, throwing and catching with the same hand. When her desire to play piano did not diminish, she steadily plucked away at the keys, burrowing through stacks of sheet music in an attempt to teach herself.

By the time she finished elementary school in 1984, her family once again experienced an expansion. Dick and Sandra adopted a one-and-a-half year old from an orphanage in the Philippines. On Halloween, the Bauer family congregated at JFK Airport as they received their newest sister, Julie-Ann, in an eager embrace.

The next few years, as her siblings played behind her on the floor of their Hampton home, Cindy continued to rehearse. For her, there was no stronger motivation to do something than when she was told she couldn't. Of late, she was buried in a piano and vocal composition titled "The Rose." She wanted to play it for her grandparents' fortieth wedding anniversary and vow renewal. The event would undoubtedly be emotional. Not only did her grandparents share a deep love for one another, but Gerard had recently been diagnosed with leukemia. The news, along with their deep attachment, motivated Cindy to resolve to be flawless.

When the day arrived, she saw her grandfather in the audience the way he often appeared at church, head bent, eyes closed, and deep in concentration. With determination, she lifted her arm and struck the first key.

CHAPTER 5

THE EQUATOR

Go out quickly into the streets and alleys of the town and bring in the poor, the crippled, the blind, and the lame.—Luke 14:21

Kenya, 1982

Leonard glanced uncomfortably around the room. His teacher was conducting a session about drainage. Rather than using the traditional lecture format, he chose to demonstrate his points in a highly unorthodox manner—by utilizing the body of a coworker like a map.

"As you can see," he illustrated, "her hair is braided in a way that represents how streams of water flow down from the mountain forming a radial drainage pattern."

He then told the students to rise and use their bodies to represent a map of Africa. The breast marked the Tropic of Cancer, the waist the Equator, and the knees the Tropic of Capricorn. He then began to talk about the climate and vegetation in each region.

"For example," he said, "if a female student was to touch her breast, it would feel hot and dry. This is just like the Sahara Desert."

When he started asking about the climate and vegetation in the area around the waist, the students exchanged looks with one another.

"Most likely, the climate is hot and wet with a high humidity. There would probably be a dense forest in this equatorial region," explained one of the students.

A stifled giggle broke out from another student. Nobody could understand why the teacher was choosing such an unconventional approach.

As Leonard later learned, his instructor spent much of his time working with blind students and was used to illustrating his statements in a tangible way. Leonard had to admit—it certainly made for a memorable lesson!

Over the next few years, he pored over his private studies to receive his A-Level Certificate, a prerequisite for attending special-needs college. While his career plans continued to progress, his personal life was still at a stalemate. He knew Janet was finished with her schooling, so he mustered the courage and went to speak with her once again.

With unexpected pleasure, Janet discovered a place growing in her heart for Leonard. Within six months of seeking her out, he not only befriended her again, but one night he stood beside her as her brothers carried her belongings to a meeting place at the perimeter of the village. It was December 31. When New Year's 1987 arrived, they were husband and wife.

The next day they celebrated with their friends and family while singing, dancing, and slaughtering two goats. Meanwhile, Leonard's mother and uncle brought cash and two female goats to Janet's parents as a bride price.

Janet and Leonard in 2010

Over time, Janet found that Leonard not only refrained from extinguishing her aspirations, he actively encouraged them. She proceeded to take a two-year course in teaching that allowed her to work at a local nursery school. Meanwhile, Leonard completed two additional years in college, receiving training in special education. Since the Ministry of Education did not offer him training to major in hearing or visual impairment, he concentrated on other physical disabilities. Hoping to expand his teaching portfolio, he decided to embrace the opportunity.

Ultimately, his experiences, along with his other credentials, helped him advance in his career. By 1993, he was awarded a position at the Assessment Center in Kilifi, the primary place to work when identifying children with disabilities in the community. Typically he identified children with disabilities every school term by talking with village chiefs, school staff, parents, friends, and neighbors in the community. He asked anyone with knowledge of a child with a disability to bring him or her to the nearby school to be assessed.

On assessment days, Leonard stood at the designated school grounds while parents and guardians brought their children forward one by one. For some people, this meant carrying the child on their backs, the only form of mobility available. Other children propelled their bodies forward by dragging themselves across the ground. Since isolation was the only thing most of them had experienced, the assessment represented the first time they had ventured out in public.

As each child was brought before him, Leonard jotted down notes. It was an almost insurmountable task. As he spent a couple of minutes with each child, he tried to identify years' worth of needs. Not only was it his responsibility to roughly speculate on their condition but to refer emergency cases to medical authorities, follow up with families at their homes to determine possible school placement, offer counseling to parents, and to educate the community on disabilities. What he often found, however, was that parents were frequently not accessible and that the resources for medical treatment and education were meager at best. It seemed fruitless to bear witness to the condition of these children without the hope of offering them any respite from their circumstance. He struggled to find sense in the social structure around him and the tools to do something about it.

In the unpredictable environment around him, he longed for the provision of something greater. Through the course of his marriage with Janet, he taught her the value of people with disabilities, such as the value of people like her brother, who was unnecessarily killed. Even Janet's mother admitted she would not take the same action against her younger brother if she had it to do over. She had seen what people with disabilities could do and decided to leave such decisions to God.

Meanwhile, with the help of a local minister, Janet became instrumental in leading Leonard to faith. When he heard the biblical story of a rich man inviting the poor and rejected to a feast, the dissolution of social barriers appealed to the deepest parts of him. Although he had been baptized in 1971, his faith had remained dormant. When a revival arrived in town, Leonard quietly left the house to attend. Without warning to his friends or family, he accepted Christ as his Savior and began to more actively incorporate him in his life.

It was not long after that when an idea began to form in his mind. Just like the rich man in the Bible, Leonard wanted to invite the children with disabilities in his own community to be an active part of society. While attending a course on assessment, he began scribbling notes, fleshing out an idea that would one day change innumerable lives.

CHAPTER 6

THE UNCONQUERABLE ELEPHANT

The Lord does not look at the things people look at. People look at the outward appearance, but the Lord looks at the heart.—1 Samuel 16:7

Maine, 1988

Using her right hand and the tip of her left arm, Cindy knit the notes together. For her, the song was both an offering of love to her grandparents and a crucible, whereby she tested her abilities under the fiery possibility of failure. When her song concluded, she saw her grandparents beaming with pride. Finishing successfully, she returned to her seat, placing the prosthetic back on her arm. Although the device was designed to be helpful, she often found it to be more of a cosmetic accessory than an aide.

Since her childhood, her family had gone to great lengths to provide her with a slew of prosthetics correlating with her growing size and age. Driving three hours, they commuted back and forth to Shriners Hospital for Crippled Children in Springfield, a charitable hospital that provided free of charge services for children with disabilities. Each visit was an education as they witnessed an assembly line of maladies. Children in the hallway were organized in rows and visited by a cluster of doctors in white coats, asking a plethora of questions, tape recorders in hand.

One of the hardest aspects of the visit for Cindy was not the doctors or the prosthetic but the emotional turmoil that was evident in her father.

As they'd sit in the waiting room, Dick often embraced Cindy with tears in his eyes, telling her that he longed to give her his own hand.

Cindy, on the other hand, only smiled. "A man hand?" She giggled. "That would just be *weird*!"

When it was her turn, she endured the experience like going to the dentist, often being reprimanded for not wearing her prosthetic more often. By high school, however, the doctors tried a new technology. The myoelectric arm strapped on to her elbow and operated via an electrode on her skin. The electrode registered when the muscles of her upper arm flexed, processed the signal through a controller, and translated it into movement. After several fittings, the device was finally ready for use.

Standing before her, the doctor lifted his finger in front of her face. "Squeeze it," he said confidently.

Cindy glanced down at the new contraption. As she lifted the metal extension in front of his hand, she aligned the fingertips to be parallel to both sides of his. While she concentrated on flexing her arm muscles, the device suddenly clamped down forcefully on the doctor's hand. Back in the waiting room, her little brother, Andy, heard the screams. Apparently, the new arm would require some practice.

Unfortunately, it was not the first malfunction Cindy had endured. One year while skiing at Mt. Cranmore with her family, she used her poles to push off of a snowy embankment. In one swift movement she suddenly felt the left side of her body grow noticeably lighter. When she turned to look at her left arm, she observed a gaping void at the end of her sleeve. As she glanced over her shoulder, she noticed her pole triumphantly staked in the snow with the prosthetic still attached like a banner in the wind. As she frequently realized, prosthetics simply didn't operate like natural limbs.

When a prosthetic wasn't getting in her way, she found she was very athletic. In soccer, she managed to land in the newspaper in an article titled "Bauer Power," boasting of her powerful force as a sweeper back for her school's team. She also excelled in a number of other activities, such as all-state chorus and advanced academics. At one point, the school even called her parents to recruit her as a trumpet player for their notable jazz band. Although she eventually declined the invitation, her interest in music remained undiminished.

When Christmas rolled around, the fifteen-year-old pleaded with her parents to buy her a guitar. Although Dick and Sandra did not know how Cindy might play it, the stringed instrument lay wrapped beneath the tree on Christmas morning nonetheless. With her typical ingenuity, Cindy found a way to adapt. While at her gram's house, Cindy rigged together a contraption that helped her play. By turning a Dixie paper cup over the tip of her left arm, she was able to insert a pick into the cardboard and strum. It was just one more activity where removing her prosthetic actually made a task easier to complete.

As the hassle of the false limb mounted, Cindy ultimately decided to wear it less and less. Although it was an advantageous tool for battering her siblings, she found she was able to do and feel much more without it.

At sixteen, Cindy started formal lessons with her guitar. Her teacher introduced her to another musician who was excited, rather than put off, by teaching her advanced piano skills. By instructing her on chord structure and an improvisational approach, he taught Cindy how to adapt written music by moving some of the left-handed notes to her right hand. With this technique, she was able to pick out the keys that were feasible to play and often produce an even fuller sound.

While she continued to improve in her music, another area of her life began to suffer. Cindy's grandfather continued to deteriorate. She often visited him in Maine, relishing the hours spent playing board games and talking. When Gerard lost his ability to speak, Cindy sang to him at his bedside while he squeezed her hand.

In the summer of 1990 when he passed, it came as no surprise that he managed to be inspirational even in his death. Before he lost the ability to speak, Gerard had recorded a sermon. On the day of his funeral, the sermon was played to an overflowing crowd that extended onto the front lawn. During the program, Cindy also sang and played Taps on her trumpet.

As time went on, Cindy often thumbed through the book of memories that her grandfather left her. In it was a letter.

"To Cindy, my first grandchild,

"Maybe you never realized it, but you have been a great help and inspiration to me. You have brought so much love to me and Grammie. I am so proud of you and your Christian faith. It gives me great joy to listen to you play and sing. God has given you some special talents, and I know you will use them wisely and for the glory of God.

"Always remember that a beautiful garden is the result of sunshine and of rain. All sunshine makes a desert. Learn and grow stronger from the storms of life, and that will make the sunshine warmer and beautiful.

"Always remember, Cindy, that as long as I live here on Earth, I will always love you. After I get to heaven I will still continue to love you.

"Grampy Wilbur"

Her grandfather challenged her to live up to the potential he recognized in her. Utilizing their shared interest, she decided to attend the University of Maine as a student in their prestigious wildlife program.

Within months of her arrival, she found herself deluged with new friendships. Her intelligence, quick laugh, and nothing-is-off-limits conversation style made her attractive—especially to one person in particular. A male student was seated right next to her in her biology class. As they began to talk to each other more and more, she felt herself growing increasingly anxious that they had never discussed her arm. Until it was acknowledged, it remained an unconquerable elephant in the room.

CHAPTER 7

RAISING STONES

Wisdom is like the baobab tree; no one individual can embrace it.—African Proverb

Kenya, 1998

As Leonard sat on the plane, he glimpsed the familiar baobab trees. According to ancient folklore, the Great Spirit gave a tree to all the animals of the earth, with the exception of the hyena. The hyena was told that unless his behavior changed and he stopped stealing from the other animals, he would not receive a tree. Eventually, the Great Spirit gave in to the impatient hyena and gave him the very last tree—the baobab. In a fit of anger, the hyena planted the seedling upside down, creating its unusual stature and causing it to look like it had roots for limbs.

As Leonard looked out his window at the trees, he was grateful to see the Kenyan landscape stretching out before him. He was returning from a course in Denmark on assessing disabilities. At the time, Denmark was a large supporter of special-needs education in Kenya. During the trip, both he and his companions saved their daily stipend to use back home. Instead of buying their meals in Denmark, many of them chose to pack rice and beans from home.

With all their weighty provisions, the taxi driver at the airport struggled to help them with their baggage. In exasperation, the attendant exclaimed, "You must have brought all the stones from Kenya!"

Leonard silently thanked himself for his foresight in packing his favorite food, a grainy cornmeal dish called *ugali*. He didn't want to think about going almost two months without it!

After six weeks of training in Denmark, he was finally able to return home. He looked forward to seeing Janet and their three children: their ten-year-old son, Victor, their five-year-old daughter, Lucky, and their youngest son, who was nothing short of a miracle. During his wife's pregnancy with his youngest, Janet was carrying twins, although only the firstborn survived. When she held the remaining child in her arms, she noticed that the baby did not appear to be in good health. After consulting multiple doctors and slowly nursing him back to health, they decided to name him after the assistance they received. His name simply became "Doctor." The second born, Rodgers, died of malaria at seven months.

In addition to seeing his family, Leonard also planned to start a new position at work. In the past he had helped establish special schools for children with disabilities, including the Sir Ali School, the Kakoneni School, and the Takaye School.

Over the past few years, Leonard also devoted his spare time to assessing numerous children with disabilities in his hometown. He was trying to gather additional research for his new idea. He had mapped out what he thought was the perfect location for a small home, a place where children with disabilities were able to attend school and board overnight when they lived too far away or lacked mobility. All of the factors were ideal for its placement, including its location at the junction of major roads and its access to medical care and water. As he gathered files on the children he assessed nearby, he wondered how to go about raising money to establish his dream.

To his astonishment, it was not long before his boss received a phone call from the District Education Office. Coincidentally, the government was looking for a place where more than ten children were assessed with the same disability. The Danish government wanted to donate funds to help children with special needs. When Leonard eagerly reported on his work in the Gede (pronounced Geddy) area, the government seized the opportunity to help establish one of eight small homes in the country.

In the past, the Kenyan government never provided people with disabilities with assistance or education of any kind. Before the country's independence from British rule in 1963, those fortunate enough to receive an education were sent to separate special schools established by missionaries or to private Catholic homes. Even after independence, the government simply did not have enough funds to create the number of special schools needed to accommodate all the demand. Therefore, when Denmark, like other funding countries, offered them aid, the government decided to establish a small home using Leonard's predetermined location. This placement was adjacent to the mainstream elementary school in town, the Gede School. Not only did this allow for children with disabilities to integrate into mainstream society, it defrayed a large portion of building costs since they shared some of their space and materials.

Since the district was recently split into two, Leonard was delegated to establish an assessment center in the new Malindi District. His office was a tiny room at the Gede School compound. It included a small desk, two chairs, and an insufficient source of sunlight from two barred windows. Since the room was also used for food storage, Leonard could only occupy a fraction of its space. From his office, he watched the Gede Small Home open its doors to a handful of children with disabilities. Although the home boasted room for twenty children, he discovered that most of them lacked the resources to pay for the boarding fees, which included costs for housemother care, water, and electricity.

Yet another disappointment was the lack of food. Since neither the government nor the parents were able to fund food for the children, the students at the small home depended entirely on well-wishers. In fact, it was not uncommon for the children to go without meals altogether. Whenever possible, the area chief divvied up relief food. Additionally, one of the teachers, Gabriel, took the initiative to travel throughout town begging for food. He visited various tourist sites, such as the Gede Ruins (an excavation site for the remains of the Swahili town dating back to the twelfth century), Kipepeo (a local butterfly farm), the trading center, and many other locations. It was the head of Kipepeo, though, who finally took pity on the children. The manager donated some money while the area chief provided relief food including sacks of maize and bales of beans to prevent the children from starving. Due to their generosity, the children were able to eat for the next month.

Another challenge was the lack of parent involvement. Many of the parents neglected to take their children back to school after the holidays. Since the children were not able to make the journey on their own, they were often left at home until someone at the school took the time to enquire after them.

Furthermore, many of the parents lacked the resources to provide medical assistance. This included medications for the children's conditions as well as professional care from nurses and occupational therapists. In fact, just recently a child fell from a tree while visiting his home and was rushed to the hospital. When he returned to Gede, it was apparent that his spine was injured and the condition was very difficult to manage. The child was withdrawn from the school and sent home, but the lack of care he received there caused him to develop enormous bed sores that became septic and ultimately led to his death. It was a source of grief for Leonard and for all those at the small home. It seemed that, for so many reasons, survival was a daily struggle.

Leonard also experienced frustration from the lack of available classrooms. While two classes of deaf students were able to borrow a room from the mainstream school, those with more severe physical disabilities did not have anywhere to go. Leonard, unable to watch two such children relegated to the margins of society yet again, decided to take them into his own office. In the already-confined space, he made room for the beginnings of a classroom. Although the materials were modest, he knew this arrangement was still preferable to these children than the neglect or abuse they likely received at home.

One of these children, Rashid, suffered from an irregular walking gait because his legs were different sizes and the arch of his foot was high, hollow, and unable to support his weight. At the tender age of six, he also experienced hemiparesis (a weakness on one side), atrophied muscles, and a condition called hydrocephalus. His tiny, palsied frame struggled to support his weighty head, engorged from an abnormal collection of cerebrospinal fluid in the brain. Back in his single-parent home, his mother often left him alone for hours while she went to the market to sell her merchandise. Unfortunately, it was not often that she earned enough for the food they needed. Meanwhile, the neighboring children teased him and hit him on his head.

At the school, while Rashid missed his mother who loved him very much, he also found refuge. The tiny child adored singing quietly, never having to have to go to sleep alone, and living in community with other children with disabilities. For Leonard, he was one more reason to find a way to build proper classrooms. There were countless other children like Rashid living in unimaginable circumstances, just waiting to be found and given an opportunity.

He set to work investigating the possibilities for special classrooms and discovered that the best place was the structure nearest to the small home. Unfortunately, the antiquated building was a historical landmark, making it illegal to demolish. While Leonard campaigned to use the space, he also searched for financial backing. Fortunately, he was able to convince the local development committee to allow him to renovate the building for the sake of the children.

Furthermore, since the Gede School was located near a strip of British and Italian beach resorts, he solicited a rotary club of expatriates accustomed to helping with community projects. As he laid out his plan, he took note of their reluctance. Patiently, he explained that it was best for the children to be educated near their homes. Casting them off only segregated them further.

The Rotarians mulled over his reasoning before coming to agreement. They agreed to renovate the building to create one classroom for the deaf and one for students with physical disabilities. Leonard's heart leapt in celebration, although reality soon set in once again. Just a short while later he experienced a confrontation with an education officer from the government. The officer, tired of the small home's constant pleas for resources, threatened to remove it altogether.

"This small home is beginning to become a problem," the education officer stated. "These children are always needing food and assistance, and we are constantly being bothered with demands for their well-being."

Although usually the monument of decorum, Leonard felt his face become an oven of irritability.

The officer continued. "The children at the small home are too taxing. They are taking away too many resources from our other programs for feeding. Perhaps it is best to remove the small home altogether."

Leonard, finally losing his patience, interjected firmly, "I believe these children are here to stay."

His eyes swept the room, holding each face accountable. "If you don't support the children, God himself will raise stones to support these children."

The education officer stared at him as Leonard added, "You and I will go, but the children will be here forever."

Leonard took his seat—and let the silence reorder their hearts.

CHAPTER 8

PILLAR OF CLOUD

By day the Lord went ahead of them in a pillar of cloud to guide them.—Exodus 13:21

Somewhere over the Atlantic Ocean, 1995

Cindy sat wedged in the middle of a five-seat row on the airplane, flanked by an obese man obstructing her access to the aisle and bathroom. For the duration of the trip, she endured her discomfort until she arrived in London to meet up with a team of volunteers. All of them were involved with Global Missions Outreach, an organization she discovered while attending a missions conference called Urbana. The team of seven people convened in the United Kingdom before departing on a ten-hour flight, this time to their final destination of Kachunga Village, Uganda.

By the time they landed and began the six-hour drive, Cindy already dreaded the effort needed to get back home. She tucked her body sleepily on top of a pile of luggage while the vehicle plowed through the dusty roads ahead. When she woke, she surveyed her new surroundings. Despite its unfamiliarity, she felt oddly at home.

For the next week, the team focused on evangelism. They set off from hut to hut in the highly populated Muslim area sharing their testimonies through a translator, showing films, and playing music. Along the way, they gained many converts to Christianity.

As they drove down the roads, the children ran after them, greeting them in their native tongue. "Jambo! Jambo!" they cried.

In response, the leader of the group stuck her head out of the window, screaming, "Jesus loves you!" to Cindy's great chagrin.

She didn't understand the point of hurling out platitudes when the children did not speak their language and needed so much more than a cursory exclamation. She sat with the unsettling feeling that there was a better way to transform the lives of these people. During their visits to various homes, she observed people with red-tinged hair, a marked sign of a critical iron deficiency. Other Ugandans' bodies were marked by the ravages of AIDS, bloated bellies from malnutrition, and a host of other symptoms and illnesses. On one particular visit, she encountered a little girl with eye difficulty.

When Cindy consulted with a doctor in their group, he explained that it was a very basic and treatable ailment.

"Why can't you fix it?" she asked, astonished.

"I didn't bring my bag of supplies," he answered matter-of-factly.

Cindy, exasperated, wondered at his shortsightedness. She realized the importance of sharing Christ, but to do so while failing to meet the people's basic and immediate needs was, in her mind, nothing short of arrogant. She began to think of what they might accomplish if someone organized more than just his or her words.

Florida, 1997

After returning from her trip, she finished up her last year at the University of Maine, earning a degree in wildlife management and conservation biology. The trip to Uganda had been monumental for her, not only because she fulfilled her lifelong dream of visiting Africa but because she endeavored past the heartache she experienced the year before. After dating her friend for two years and even discussing marriage, she eventually became discouraged about his lack of enthusiasm for missions. Although they decided to separate, Cindy was still unsettled by the discovery that he had moved on to dating and eventually marrying her roommate. She also feared that his level of comfort with her arm condition was solely because his grandmother had one arm. She worried that other men wouldn't be as understanding and wouldn't have a desire to marry her. Devastated, she returned home and continued her credits locally at the University of New

Hampshire and Gordon College. The trip to Uganda had been a personal conquest to aid other people and repair her own heart.

Now that she successfully finished her degree, she undertook the daunting task of finding employment. After going home and exploring a number of options, she ultimately decided to pursue a series of wildlife jobs in Florida. This helped her gain the experience she needed for graduate school.

Her first position was at the Florida Panther National Wildlife Refuge. For the next year she jet-setted around the perimeter of the swamp on her four wheeler. At night she stayed in a tiny camper that was so small she was not able sit up straight in the bedroom. When her contract was up, she took a job at the Corkscrew Swamp and Sanctuary.

Florida seemed to offer an endless list of wildlife jobs. Her encounters with alligators and other poisonous insects did not seem to faze her a bit, and she enjoyed spending more of a relaxed time with the kids during the children's tours she led. After a string of jobs, however, she decided it was best to return home and take a handful of graduate classes while teaching on the side.

Despite her busy schedule, she still longed for something more meaningful. She worried that a thousand everyday decisions might ultimately lead her astray from doing something that truly mattered, like doing conservation work in Africa. She remembered the advice from her pastor and family friend while she was in Florida. He explained that sometimes the waiting period is itself a calling. Even Moses followed a pillar of cloud that sometimes stood still.

To Cindy's delight, it was not long before her pillar of cloud did indeed begin to move. In just a short period of time, she encountered one of her old professors, Dr. Wright, who told her of an upcoming program connected to Au Sable, the environmental conservation center she once attended while earning her final undergraduate credits. As she learned, Au Sable just established a new branch—and this one was nestled a continent away, deep in the heart of Africa.

Kenya, 1999

"I had a farm in Africa at the foot of the Ngong Hills."

Cindy shaped Meryl Streep's words in her head from one of her favorite films, *Out of Africa*. For two months she took wildlife classes at the foot of the Ngong Hills among a tribal Masai village, desiring to be like one of her two heroines, Dian Fossey and Jane Goodall. Every other week she took courses on mammalogy and sustainable agriculture. During the intervening weeks, the students traveled on buses to safari parks all over the country.

Her first day of safari was in Amboseli National Park by Mt. Kilimanjaro. Her first night was anything but peaceful. In the morning her friend had looked at her and responded wearily, "That was the worst night of my life."

Cindy laughed in understanding. The group didn't stay in luxurious and fenced-in accommodations but in thin tents inside the park itself. As the students slept, a vast wilderness awoke around them. By listening to the sounds, they identified lively narratives of predators audibly chewing their prey, sometimes wondering which category they fell into. They also detected a plethora of twig snapping, as if the world around them was one big inhospitable wicker chair.

When Cindy needed to leave the comfort of her tent to relieve her bladder, the beam of her flashlight captured pairs of eyes of glittering back at her. In fact, one day she had to pitch her tent next to a large set of leopard prints. She immediately visualized the untimely demise of Tarzan's parents by a leopard in the 1999 Disney movie *Tarzan*.

On another occasion, the students set up camp beside Lake Naivasha, when she discovered a hippo grazing around the perimeter of her tent. Notoriously dangerous, she was left with no other choice than to wait it out until the animal finally migrated elsewhere.

Even when she was taking classes in an urban area, there was no shortage of unsettling elements. In Nairobi, she was unable to take her eyes off the hordes of beggars. Moved by their poverty, she bought one family rice and milk, which only caused her to be mobbed by others wanting the same thing. When she discussed the encounter with her friends, she was dismayed at their ability to quickly dismiss the suffering that surrounded them. Cindy contemplated how she might prevent her heart from becoming calloused. As she observed, many of the people begging were people with disabilities. During one particularly meaningful encounter, she met a man pleading for change. She couldn't help but notice something familiar—the marked absence of his left hand.

As Cindy discussed the man's condition with one of her professors, she learned about the local views about people with disabilities being considered cursed. She was even further disturbed by his next response. In no uncertain terms, her professor told her, "If you had been born in Kenya, you would likely have been killed."

CHAPTER 9

A FOOL'S ERRAND

In their hearts humans plan their course, but the Lord establishes their steps. —Proverbs 16:9

Kenya, June 2000

"Her name was *Lo*la. She was a *show*girl."

Willy's Kenyan accent underscored his singing as he proudly donned his red Copacabana T-shirt. Until Cindy's arrival, he was unconscious of the fact that a show tune corresponded with his favorite apparel. On his head rested a soiled, khaki baseball hat that framed his smiling eyes. Next to his slight, twenty-eight-year-old frame stood Cindy, a few inches taller, her hair tied back in the triangle of her bandana and her cut-off pants stained red with forest dirt at the knees.

Her voice conspired with his, and the crunch of their footsteps started to match their short, staccato lines. "At the *Co*pa" (crunch!), "Copaca*ban*a" (crunch! crunch!), "the hottest spot north of—"

Willy froze as Cindy abruptly crashed into his backside. An animal the size of a small rabbit with dark fur and a conspicuous golden patch on its hindquarters scurried across the path and into the leaves ahead. Cindy swung her bag around and pulled out her notebook to document the line of transect. Just a year ago she decided to investigate the now endangered golden-rumped elephant shrew, or the *fugu*, as it was termed locally. The tiny, rodent-like animal looked like an anteater in miniature. Its long, flexible nose was put to use sifting through leaves on the forest floor as it ran on tiny legs, its head bent downward with mouselike ears. The species was only found deep in the heart of the Arabuko Sokoke Forest in Kenya. The acreage of wildlife they called home represented the largest coastal forest in eastern Africa, spanning 260 square miles about an hour north of the major port city, Mombasa.

Cindy first decided to study the animal when she enrolled at Eastern Kentucky University for a master's in applied ecology. A contact from her time at Au Sable told her about research opportunities in the Arabuko Sokoke forest. Today, only half the extensive habitat remained. Over the last twenty years, the demand for firewood and woodcarvings continued to decimate the forest. Since the fugu was endemic to the forest, it was a useful indicator species to help gauge overall ecosystem health. Studying its nests was an easy way of determining how the population was affected by human interaction in the area. She was especially drawn to discovering balances between environmental and social issues.

From June through August, Willy and Cindy battled the native vines and greenery to discover the fugu's leafy nests. Working alongside one another like siblings, they plowed through the thick vegetation, sometimes crawling in pursuit on hands and knees. Meanwhile, the fugu blissfully spent its day rooting through debris on the forest floor, prowling about for grasshoppers, spiders, and other invertebrates.

Although Cindy and Willy now patterned their moves together in smooth synchronization, things had started out rather precariously. On her first day in the forest, Willy and Cindy had waited for the other to speak first. He had never been asked to assist with finding the strange animal nest before. In fact, locally the fugu was considered a bad omen, akin to a black cat. Although some local children hunted the animal for recreation and set up makeshift traps, most adults avoided the fugu altogether. Even more damaging to its reputation was the stigma that it was considered very foolish. When the fugu was startled by a human, the rodent-like animal darted off, only to forget about the recent source of danger within moments. It was so notorious for its bouts of amnesia that the locals considered the effect to be contagious if you ate its meat. This was the animal that a *mzungu*, a white person, came halfway around the world to study.

While Willy refrained from questioning her motives, he was still unsure where to begin. Furthermore, he was concerned how Cindy would manage trekking through the forest for eight hours a day in extreme conditions. She was the first female to ask for his assistance through the forest. In his experience, even strong men found it difficult to maneuver through the untamed recesses. An awkward first morning ensued while the pair aimlessly wandered around. Cindy waited for Willy to take charge while Willy waited for instruction from Cindy. When she finally spoke up, a look of relief spread across the corners of his face.

Cindy's battle plan was to locate the fugu's nests by segmenting the forest into plots and traversing them at random paths of intersection called "transect lines." By avoiding the tourist trails, the pair might gather data samples at random and record more accurate results. The protective leaf piles were easy to identify because their perimeter was scooped bare. The fugu piled leaves from the forest floor into small mounds about a half a foot tall and a little less than two feet across. When a nest was found within ten feet of the transect line, Cindy carefully documented its location. The pair quickly exhausted themselves covering large territories of the forest floor. As the two progressed, so did Willy's impression of Cindy's capabilities. Not only did she endure the harsh elements well, she endured it *better* than most men.

For the next few months, Willy blazed transect lines through the intimidating green chaos, machete in hand and Cindy close behind. Generally, the days were hot and humid. The woven canopy of leaves often protected the pair from the penetration of the sun, casting a chiaroscuro effect of shadow and light onto the ground before them. When the rains came, so did a vibrating haze of flittering insects, particularly the bothersome onslaught of mosquitoes. Some insects, however, remained a threat even without the sudden downpours. Within the first few weeks of research, Willy plowed right into a hornet's nest as he furrowed through the branches before him. After multiple stings, Cindy glanced at Willy's face, which was full of exasperated indignation.

"Willy, what are you going to do?"

"I'm going to kill them all!" he fumed.

She laughed at his passionate and futile retaliation. His openness and good humor with foreigners made him a quick ally. She was fortunate to have found such a compatible accomplice for the long hours of data-gathering. Willy even invited her to share some meals with his wife and children. Their long and sometimes formidable excursions through the shrubbery allowed them to form a steadfast friendship as researcher and assistant.

His presence also protected her from a number of threats. On one July afternoon, Cindy and Willy ventured precariously close to some elephants, a skittish breed unlike those on the savannah. According to the direction of the wind, the elephants were able to detect the scent of foreigners, causing them to become remarkably territorial. Willy, well-versed in the native wildlife, was able to pick up their scent too, although Cindy was generally unable to learn the tracking skill despite her most concentrated efforts at sniffing the air. In this instance, however, her nose prickled with identification.

Willy's hand reached back and motioned for Cindy to cease movement. She paused and impatiently shifted her weight, stubbornly wishing to continue her study. Willy shook his head in vehement disapproval. The massive elephants were fiercely protective of their young, and any detection of Cindy and Willy might provoke one of the clan to charge. Chances of outrunning them over any great distance were impossible—hence Willy's rule to keep the doors to the truck unlocked. If an elephant charged, the best bet was to take refuge in the vehicle.

They carefully retraced their steps. It was easy to inadvertently wander into reptile-infested bramble.

"How will we get back?" Cindy whispered.

Willy replied matter-of-factly, "Very carefully."

Without another word they began their long withdrawal.

Meanwhile, their drivers waited back in the vehicle where they detected the elephants too. After several moments, the sounds grew nearer and still there was no sign of Willy or Cindy. As the minutes ticked by, the crashing noise of timber and leaves emerged from the perimeter of their path. They watched in consternation as the elephants broke through the foliage and meandered across the road, eventually disappearing altogether.

Many minutes later, Cindy and Willy returned to their forest vehicle. As they finally climbed in, they found their drivers staring at them. As they set out again, Cindy remembered another piece of Willy's advice. She turned, looked to her right, and quickly rolled up her window. The closed glass helped block the poisonous spit of cobras. The treacherous reptile was able to shoot venom straight in your eyes with deadly accuracy. As the truck drove through the dirt-scored path, the tires kicked up a final cloud of dust in their wake. Thanks to Willy's protection, Cindy managed to persevere through one more day in the wild unscathed.

In the evenings, she found safe haven at Mrs. Simpson's Guest House, where she lodged. Although there were frequent visitors from other corners of the world, she often found that the isolation from home still caused her to feel alone. A couple of times, the palpable loneliness almost overcame her commitment to the work, and she considered returning to the United States. Everything seemed to require more effort than she anticipated. Her visa arrived just two days before her departure. Her laptop broke within days of her arrival. In fact, she only recently acquired any steady means of transportation. As she drove, people would shout "Ciao!" to her, assuming she was an Italian tourist. Nothing seemed to go as planned. As she wrote in her journal, "I am in a very random place, doing a very random work. I wonder what the ultimate purpose is!"

At the end of each evening, she returned to her modest whitewashed room. She slept under a mosquito net while the monkeys battled each other, throwing seeds on the corrugated tin roof. In the morning she would drive back to the forest, passing a small cluster of buildings that always caught her attention. On the side was written in black paint "Gede Home for the Physically Handicapped."

When she enquired about it to Willy one day during their field work, he had looked up at her with a knowing smile. "I can do better than tell you what it is," he replied. "I can take you there."

CHAPTER 10

COMPASS FOR COMPASSION

Speak up for those who cannot speak for themselves, for the rights of all who are destitute. —Proverbs 31:8

Kenya, July 4, 2000

Cindy watched as her driver continued to weave around potholes, bicycles, and the bustle of stray livestock. She felt as if the obstacles in their path, in conjunction with the driver's well-timed swerves, were like a video game. They picked up another passenger, a representative from the Turtle Bay Resort, and made their way down the road in Watamu that ran parallel to the British and Italian resorts lining the waterfront. Her friend hoped to investigate charity opportunities for the hotel where he worked while Cindy simply hoped to find out more about the place she passed each day on her way to the forest.

Maneuvering through the crowded street, lurching from potholes and makeshift speed bumps, they passed vendors in their shops until they pulled up to the school's entrance. A guard opened the gate to give her access, and within seconds, she spotted her field guide, Willy, already waiting. Jumping out of the truck, Cindy and her friend greeted him warmly.

To the right of the dirt driveway was an L-shaped row of classrooms that belonged to the mainstream Gede School. From the square window openings carved into the concrete and coral block buildings she heard the voices of children reciting their lessons. Glancing in their direction, she saw that they were dressed in their school uniforms: blue button-down shirts, shorts for the boys, and skirts for the girls. Each child sat at a worn wooden desk before a chalkboard, the writing barely visible by the sunlight struggling to illuminate the shady rooms.

To the left of the driveway was the designated area for the special school. Willy brought her to the assessment center's office and introduced her to his cousin, Leonard. From his tiny work space, she took a seat and signed the guest book spread out before her. As with most places she visited in Kenya, formalities were of the utmost importance, particularly when it came to signing the guest book.

As Leonard watched her sign, he took stock of the person before him. Although it was unusual for an outsider and *mzungu*, or white person, to show interest in the school, he observed the absence of her left arm, silently wondering if her own disability gave her an internal compass for compassion. Optimistically, he offered to give her a tour of the work being done. The children were in school because the Kenyan school year ran from January to December, divided into three terms of three months each followed by a break. Starting beside his office, he showed her the small home he helped establish in 1997. Split into male and female sides, the home was lined with metal bunk beds and mosquito nets. Adjacent to the sleeping area was a row of sinks and stalls. Inside the stalls were holes in the ground that served as toilets, followed by a couple of spigots for taking showers, depending on the status of the area's water supply.

Next they visited two special-needs classrooms running perpendicular to the small home. The first was for the children who were deaf. According to an American surgeon who worked at a hospital in Nairobi, approximately 80 percent of deafness in the country was the result of preventable conditions. One child, Everlyn, was deaf after suffering from otitis media, an infection of the middle ear, a condition that 75 percent of children experience at least once by their third birthday. Unable to get treatment, her hearing deteriorated.

The other classroom they visited was for children with other physical disabilities. Approximately fifteen children were enrolled in the special school. Those fortunate enough to excel were eventually integrated into the mainstream school. At both locations, however, the teachers struggled for space. It was not uncommon for them to divide the classrooms into two different levels by using a small partition. Yet another challenge was the shortage of staff. Sometimes teachers were required to teach two classes simultaneously, allowing for only half the lessons to be taught each day. While this was not uncommon in schools throughout the country, this was even worse in a special school where each child varied dramatically in their developmental abilities.

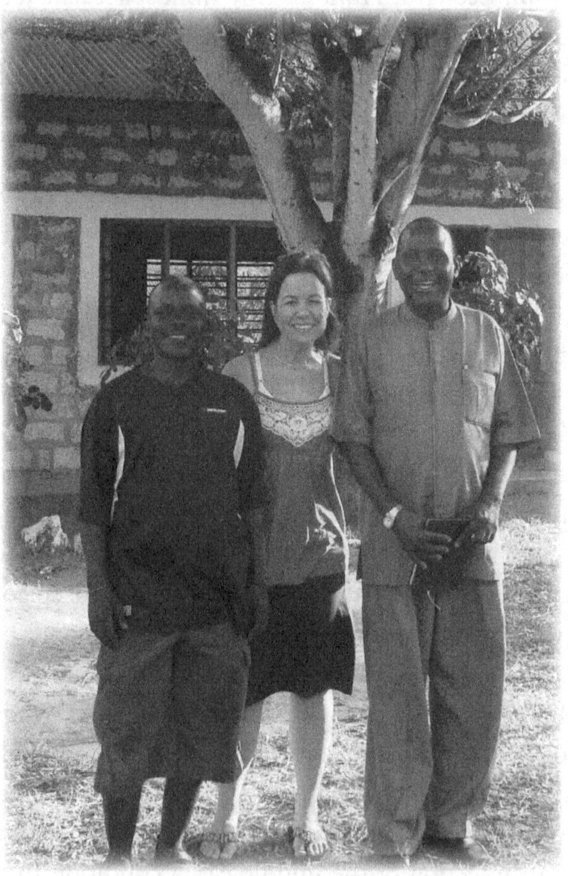

Willy, Cindy, and Leonard in front of
the Gede Special School in 2011.

As Cindy was instructed, no systematic survey had ever been done to identify and determine the exact number of children with disabilities in the area. A rapid assessment conducted by the United Nations estimated that 10 percent of Kenyan children had a disability of some sort, with only 10 percent of that figure actually attending school. Observing the children, she couldn't help but smile at their eagerness to see a visitor. Occasionally she stopped to shake one of their hands or wave hello. Each acknowledgement or touch she gave seemed to trigger a ray of light within them.

When Leonard described the conditions of these children's homes, she understood why they responded with such enthusiasm. For many of them, their community considered their disability a curse from God. Even their own parents believed their child's disability was a punishment or the result of a neighbor's curse. Other parents reacted to their child's disability with divorce, abandonment, mistreatment, neglect, or even murder. With little or no means to defend themselves, many of the children were preyed upon or generally ignored. Those with intellectual impairments were sometimes tied to trees to prevent them from wandering off. They were almost never given an education. While school fees were often difficult to pay for the average child, those with disabilities needed to pay additional fees to board and receive special care. The poverty in the area only heightened the limits placed on them.

Although Kenya was comprised of more than forty distinct tribes, one common feature among them was their view of disabilities. Although some of the most harmful practices of child elimination, often through suffocation or drowning, reduced with time, a remnant still held on to such practices. In the northeast of Kenya, nomadic tribes found mobility challenges to be particularly burdensome to their need to follow migrating herds. Along the coastal region where Leonard worked, there were nine tribes referred to as the *Mijikenda*. Each of them was heavily influenced by superstition and witchcraft.

In the country as a whole, Kenya made any form of discrimination illegal in their constitution created in 1969. However, the document was drafted in a hurry to appease pressure from human-rights activists and donor communities that they depended heavily upon. Not dissimilar from a number of other countries throughout the world, the words of the Kenyan constitution concerning equality of all people were often not paired with practice.

As Leonard began to describe the countless children with disabilities unable to be rescued or to attend the school, Cindy's interest was aroused. She asked him, "Can I meet some of them?"

They agreed to schedule a time to visit some of these children in their respective homes.

As she waited for her next appointment with Leonard, Cindy looked forward to seeing her sister, Minna, who was arriving to keep her company for a bit. When Cindy took her to the forest, the two girls showed Willy how to do "The Limbo" as they contorted in backbends under the tree limbs. Minna, an artist at heart, also added to the entertainment by weaving together wreaths of leafy halos. Willy, seeing her interest, showed her some of the native uses for the fauna around them. Slicing deep into the covering of the morning glory vine, he let his finger catch the milky sap that protruded in beads from his incision. When the sap hardened, he inserted a reed where his finger marked a hole. As he blew air into the reed, the sap ballooned out into a sphere. By adding more layers and letting it harden, the sphere became an effective, bouncy rubber ball.

Eventually, when it was time for Cindy to visit Leonard again, she took Minna along with her. With Leonard's direction, they hired a driver to take them to the children's homes. When they ventured out into the bush, it often seemed as if there wasn't a road where Leonard instructed the driver to turn. What looked like a bunch of foliage might easily be a narrow and well-camouflaged path to someone's home. She cringed hearing the tree branches scraping along the sides of the vehicle.

When they arrived, she found that most of the children lived in mud huts, frequently in deplorable conditions. They found one child named Charo Shida who was barely able to communicate. After being born with a hearing impairment and going on to develop epilepsy and various autistic behaviors, his father passed away and his mother soon abandoned him. Living with his grandparents, he struggled to survive and often begged on the street. When Cindy and Leonard visited, he managed to understand that they were from a local school that he had attended until he could no longer pay school fees. In utter delight, he ran to his hut and returned with a bag and shirt over his shoulder, hoping to be taken with them. Heartbroken by the child with the magnificent smile, Cindy was unable to take him with her. Without the resources to pay for school fees, he was relegated to the isolation of his home without the opportunity to pursue his goals for the future.

Another child they found was a girl named Dhahabu. The child was covered in scabies and so malnourished that she was unable to swallow her food.

With a heavy heart, Cindy felt her conscience unsettle. Taking pictures to document the children and their conditions, she worked out an agreement with her contact at the Turtle Bay Resort. If she was able to raise money for even a handful of the twenty-six or so children she'd met, the money could be wired to the charity account at the resort. This was an option a friend of hers who had lived in Kenya had suggested. Her contact at the hotel would then give the money directly to the headmaster of the special school. This would make an enormous difference in an area where, for more than half the population, the average daily wage was around one dollar.

As soon as she got home, she sent some of her own money to sponsor Charo Shida. She simply didn't know how to convince others to care about the remaining children who lived in such a tiny, remote dot on the map. She also didn't know of anyone more worthy of love than children, in poverty, oppressed under a stigma that often prevented people from seeing beyond the condition of their bodies to the beauty of their souls. Within months, however, she received her answer.

CHAPTER 11

COUNTERACTING THE CURSE

On the contrary, those parts of the body that seem to be weaker are indispensable. —1 Corinthians 12:22

Kenya, 2001

"Surely if I'd had this knowledge before, my brother would not have been killed," Janet admitted.

Having finished her two-year teaching course, Janet was certified in 2001 to work with children with special needs. For her first post, Cindy gathered donations to help hire her to work with the children with cerebral palsy at the Gede Special School. One of the most memorable children Janet encountered there suffered from a cleft palate, the same disability that precipitated her brother's death. This child, however, had a surgical repair—an option Janet had not known existed. In response to the tragic memory of her brother, she attempted to counteract the "curse" by caring for those with disabilities and educating her community. She realized that even more than the physical impairments the children endured, the true curse for people with disabilities lay in the response of the society around them, not in evil spirits.

One significant piece of legislation helped with providing for children with disabilities. In 2001, the Kenyan National Assembly created The Children Act, a landmark bill that endowed people with disabilities with the right to life, medical treatment, and free elementary education in an appropriate environment. Yet another positive result from the act was that it allowed single parents of children with special needs to receive financial assistance from the National Development Fund. It also allowed for the extension of parental rights after a child's eighteenth birthday. The parents were responsible for looking after their child's wellbeing by providing an adequate diet, shelter, medical care, education, and guidance. The consequence for neglecting these responsibilities was a fine of more than $2,000 or five years in prison. Although the act lacked adequate enforcement, the principle behind it was a start in the right direction.

Yet another benefit to children with disabilities at the Gede Special School in particular was the addition of a new staff member. Tall and lanky with a slight hook of the nose, Koffa—or "Doctor," as the community called him—worked three days a week doing physical therapy while being compensated by a British nurse in the area. Starting with a small mat in the corner of the children's classroom, Koffa did the combined work of a physical and occupational therapist, doctor, nurse, orthopedist, and craftsman. The need before him was so great that he often worked with multiple children at once and even missed meals to continue his assistance. When he worked with the children, he saw more than the outline of their figure. He saw the negative space around them where he wanted to equip their bodies to move.

One child he worked with, Happy, was unable to walk on his own due to his cerebral palsy. In order to get Happy to the school in the first place, his mother needed to carry him on her back through a bustling slalom of village roads. During their first encounter, Koffa noticed that Happy had charms tied around him that were traditionally used to ward off evil spirits. It was as if the bands, like puppet strings, might suddenly spur his body to movement. Koffa impatiently cut off the charms and began to do a thorough evaluation. For months he provided therapy for the child with the perpetually knit eyebrows, slowly melting the stiffness of his body into fluidity like wax. As Happy's body awakened, so did his ability to identify the sounds of friends at the school. He also began to take part in playing, laughing, eating solid food, and sitting. For months, Happy practiced these new movements, his brow furrowed into a tiny crease like a comma. It was like learning a new language he never thought he would have permission to express. By the end of his first year, he moved into uncharted territory and took his first tremulous steps. By the second year, he had moved on to fluency. He had gained total equilibrium and balance. With new ownership of his body, the child who was once carried to the school now ran into his mother's arms.

With Koffa's help, Happy was not alone in his newfound abilities. Yet another boy named Antony also arrived at the school suffering from cerebral palsy and an inability to walk. Having lived a stationary existence for years, Koffa slowly taught the boy to support himself using crutches. He was like a sprouting seed slowly asserting itself through the soil. After a lifetime of being barred from mobility, he underwent a metamorphosis that allowed him to walk and even to run. As he blossomed, he was eventually integrated into the mainstream school where he continued to flourish and move beyond the need for physical therapy altogether.

Driven by his desire to see the same results repeated in other children, Koffa felt compelled to investigating the condition of the children's homes. Without formal addresses, he rode his bicycle to the general area where the child lived and questioned neighbors until he found the correct home. In about three out of every five homes, he found single parents. Throughout Kenya disability was often a source of marital conflict. Traditionally the mother was blamed for her child's disability, often giving the husband grounds to separate.

Overall, Koffa found that home visits were the best way to learn about the background of each child and to build a relationship with the parents in order to advocate proper care. During one visit, a mother invited him into her home, where he immediately discerned that the room did not have any ventilation. The fire used for cooking sat in the middle of the living area, with no windows or chimney for the smoke to escape—a likely culprit of their child's respiratory challenges.

Another child he visited simply needed repositioning. While resting at his home, he developed a gaping bed sore that exposed his bones. It was as if the child's body had waged war against its circumstances.

Other times, he found that parents neglected to administer medication to their children. Other parents believed that all medication was similar to malaria pills and you could cease using it once your symptoms disappeared. Unfortunately, as the result of such beliefs, one child passed away from epileptic seizures while at home, the medicine that would have saved his life just mere feet away.

During all of these visits, Koffa instructed parents on appropriate care and even provided homemade assistive devices. He did everything from making equipment to helping the children do their exercises. He was like a human pocket knife with a myriad of talents. Unfortunately, more often than not, the parents did not utilize the tools he gave them. For many of these children, disability was not their only barrier. The attitudes of their caretakers also needed to be transformed. With the length of the parents' work days, their lack of resources, and high rate of illiteracy, this proved to be more than a little problematic.

Even worse was when the parents actually did attempt to care for their child but went about it in inappropriate ways. Resorting to traditional remedies, parents might hire a witch doctor to brand the child with a hot stick, believing the heat possessed healing properties. Other times parents draped a sheet over a boiled pot of herbs and the child's head, believing this created a vacuum to expel evil spirits. Another practice was to tie charms to the body. Such tactics were widespread. In fact, Koffa rarely worked with a child who did not have a history of undergoing traditional remedies.

Yet another conflict was the misunderstanding about how to prevent disabilities in the first place. Simple steps such as adequate nutrition during pregnancy, sleeping under mosquito nets, receiving immunizations, delivering at hospitals or clinics rather than at home, and avoiding traditional healers might easily avert many of the challenges the children faced.

Even Leonard's family was not immune to misunderstanding disability. One of his cousin's children, Safari, was born deaf. For many years, the boy was largely rejected by his community for his disability. As he grew older and it became time for him to attend school, he found it difficult to keep up. When his teachers complained about his pace of learning, he was ultimately forced to withdraw. From then on, he stayed at home. He was like a moth contained to a small halo of light. Most days he was left to attend to the goats and look after the property while the rest of his family worked on a farm a few miles away.

One day in 1994, Safari decided to venture away from the tedium of his confinement. Endeavoring to find his family rather than spend his days in isolation, he set out on an unknown course to track them down. On his way he passed through a scorched landscape that seemed inhospitable to even its own plant life. On the periphery were thick tangles of trees that hosted a number of other wildlife perils. With each step, he tried to hold the memory of the turns he took, but recalling them later was like trying to wring a cloud of memory out and collect the raindrops in the palm of his hand. Eventually his recollections slipped between his fingers and ultimately left him confused. Since his family had never taught him how to communicate, he did not know how to ask for directions. As time continued to slip by, the confidence he set out with digested into uncertainty. For endless hours he trekked through the wilderness, lost and disoriented until he came to a body of water where he could slake his thirst. As he waited for his family to come looking for him, the first unsettling hours gave way to days. His grip on life began to loosen as the physical effects of starvation and exposure gnawed at him.

Meanwhile, his family, alarmed when the boy went missing, began to search for him and even filed a report with the police. They combed the surrounding area but remained unsuccessful. As the days turned into a week, they grew increasingly concerned. When the police finally contacted them once again, their fears were confirmed. Safari's body had been found near Lake Jilore, just five miles away. With despair, the family was forced to identify the decomposing remains, the body providing clues about his journey like a message told in syllables. His tragic death was a period in the sentence of a life that was never able to be truly lived.

For Leonard, this was not the first time a relative had disappeared. His aunt Dzingo, who was deaf, had also disappeared in the woods many years earlier, never to be found again.

Sadly, his family was not alone in their grief. Many others with disabilities continued to struggle for a reasonable quality of life. By 2003, the international community was praising Kenya for its creation of the Persons with Disabilities Act. The legislation defined disability as "a physical, sensory, mental, or other impairment, including any visual, hearing, learning, or physical incapability, which impacts on social, economic, or environmental participation." The act proclaimed rights for people with disabilities, including the right to an education, to equal opportunities in the workplace, to medical services, to accessibility, and to be exempt from paying income tax. Despite all of its noble proclamations, however, little was being done to enforce the new guidelines. School fees were no longer necessary at mainstream schools, but children with special needs still needed money for boarding at the school and for food. While on paper Kenya had made progress, on a personal level many with disabilities still felt tormented.

CHAPTER 12

A DAY LATE AND A DOLLAR SHORT

Misfortune does not restrict his visits to one day.—African Proverb

Kenya, 2003

Returning to Kenya after three years, Cindy and her brother, Andy, met up with Leonard to assess the latest needs of children with disabilities in the area. Just a few months earlier the siblings had tried to take a volunteer group to Kenya but were prevented from doing so when all British Airways flights were shut down. Kenyan authorities had sighted a man photographing the airport—the same man who attempted to launch a shoulder-fired missile attack at a plane one year earlier. Kenya, previously known as one of the safest countries in Africa, was now red flagged. When Cindy and Andy finally arrived in Gede later in the year, they noticed that the town that depended heavily on tourism was feeling the pangs of its loss. In ill-planned desperation, a dozen or so men began using bows and arrows while robbing people. The community was enraged by the mischief but found little recourse for stopping it. Ironically, one Kenyan expressed to Cindy that he was more concerned about ever traveling to the United States, where everyone carried guns!

In spite of the warnings, the Bauer siblings plowed ahead to their destination. Cindy traveled from Maryland, where she was now working as a wildlife biologist for the Army Environmental Center. Meanwhile, her twenty-two-year-old brother, Andy, was accompanying her to see how things were operating on the ground in Kenya. He held a striking resemblance to Cindy with a naturally athletic build. At more than six feet, he looked down on Cindy with his shaved head with what was easily perceived as an intimidating presence. Yet on further acquaintance, it was his affectionate warmth, steady stream of humor, and childlike playfulness that superseded this initial impression and left people feeling like they had made a new best friend. With his interest in overseas missions and love for children, he genuinely wanted to help with Cindy's efforts.

Andy Bauer with children at the
Gede Special School in 2009.

For the past three years, Cindy had been corresponding back and forth with Leonard, who was now working full time for the Kenya Medical Research Institute (KEMRI) as a developmental assessor conducting assessments and researching the needs of children with disabilities. Since he was unaccustomed to e-mailing, he resorted to having a coworker download his e-mails every morning and print them out. While Leonard was out in the field, he read over the e-mails and wrote down his answers to Cindy's questions.

Later, his friend recorded his answers and relayed them back to the United States, where Cindy continued to speak before family and friends about the conditions of the children abroad. As she gathered more child sponsorship fees, she distributed the money to her contact at the Turtle Bay Resort, who in turn distributed it to the head teachers of the schools for emergency medical care, and for water, electricity, and food at the boarding facilities.

Eventually she decided to formalize her work. Although she did not set out to start a non-profit—in fact, she had always worked with animals in order to avoid people and the self-consciousness she sometimes experienced because of her arm condition—it seemed as if God had other plans. Wanting the name for the organization to reflect God's love for his children, she used the Kiswahili (what most non-Africans know as Swahili) word "Kupenda" (pronounced koo-PEHN-dah), roughly meaning "to love." Knowing that most Americans might not know the word "Kupenda," she contextualized it with the English phrase "for the children." For the last few years, she had been calling her efforts "Kupenda for the Children," and, when urged by a coworker, finally registered the name for nonprofit status on March 5. She also decided that she needed to return to Kenya to follow up on the status of the children and how donations were being used.

For almost two weeks Leonard took Cindy and Andy to schools throughout the district to look into the needs of children with disabilities. For almost all of the schools, the visit marked the first time someone visited to provide more than minimal help. Desperate for the assistance, each school presented a lengthy list of needs that completely overwhelmed their visitors. It was like a war of maladies in which each school competed for the most afflictions and the most aid.

At the Gede Special School, they found a scarcity of teachers. The ideal ratio of teachers to students with cerebral palsy was one to five. Yet they found two teachers and one teacher aid for twenty-four children. Recently the teachers had served thirty students; however, six students had recently integrated into the mainstream school. In the hearing-impaired classrooms, the ideal ratio of teachers to students was one to twelve, yet they found two teachers for twenty-nine children. Additionally, the teachers lacked many necessary facets to their programs, including formal curriculum, books, speech therapy, auditory training, and vocational training. At the Sir Ali School for the Mentally Handicapped, the first special school in the district established in 1994, they found forty-eight children who tried to learn vocational skills. They did this by weaving paper since they did not have the capital to buy the startup materials necessary to make baskets. At the Kakoneni Unit established in 1996, the children did not have desks and sat on the floor in dark classrooms. When they visited other schools, they encountered similar types of problems. They all seemed to be understaffed and overworked, and they lacked significant training and materials.

In the outermost part of the district they found that virtually nothing existed for children with special needs. Countrywide, Kenya officials estimated that one in every ten people had a disability. In the remote village of Marafa with a population of more than forty-four thousand, this meant more than forty-four hundred people with disabilities who lacked access to an education. The lack of any permanent water source also weakened the community's welfare. The region was semiarid and received low and unreliable amounts of rainfall. It was not uncommon for consecutive years to pass without rain, making hunger all the more rampant.

After meeting with school representatives, Cindy and Leonard decided to look into building a dormitory next to a mainstream school in hopes of establishing a small home similar to the one in Gede. Coming out of the consultation, they met hundreds of students. About fifteen hundred children attended the school, which was staffed by only twenty-four teachers. In other words, there was one teacher for every sixty-two students. Many of the children sat four to a desk if they were even fortunate enough to have one. The others simply sat on the floor.

Following them everywhere they went, Cindy and Andy soon gathered an entourage of barefoot students walking when they walked and stopping when they stopped. They were like a school of fish coordinating their movements, laughing each time at the playful synchronization.

Another heart-wrenching aspect of their trip was when they visited the homes of some of the children. They were particularly surprised that the types of disabilities they found were not common in the United States simply because such conditions were usually corrected at birth.

At one home, a little girl named Rehema suffered from spina bifida, a birth defect where her backbone and spinal canal did not close, causing a fluid-filled sac to stick out of her mid-to-lower back. At one-and–a-half years old, she also endured hydrocephalus, causing her to have an abnormal collection of cerebrospinal fluid accumulating in her brain and causing her head to enlarge, as well as other visual and intellectual impairments. Yet another child, George, also languished from hydrocephalus. His mother was widowed and unable to work. Both children were desperate for medical care in order to survive. It was apparent that the hourglasses of their lives were slipping away prematurely.

Cindy, who would shortly be departing the country, was unable to walk away from the precious children without doing something. Although she did not want to use Kupenda funds since she wouldn't be able to see to its administration directly, she left some of her personal money with the local assessment officer for the children to be taken to the hospital.

At the end of their district tour, Cindy, Andy, and Leonard discussed possible solutions for addressing all of the needs. Leonard agreed to form a community-based organization called the Malindi District Special Education Rehabilitation Organization (MADISERO) with its own bank account, rather than having to use the one at the Turtle Bay Resort. The organization was originally established by a group of special-needs teachers, but it was no longer active. Reactivating the group, Leonard hoped to create buy-in from teachers, assessment officials, and others. The group was made up of Leonard, a local pastor (Rev. Robert Mangi), a teacher (Gabriel Mwnengo) for the deaf at the Gede Special School, an assessment officer (Zurhura Masemo), and other special-needs teachers in the district.

The Kenyan educators and practitioners organized their efforts in order to report the most accurate needs for children with disabilities to the United States and subsequently a large donor population. MADISERO's input allowed for the group to take ownership of the direction development was taking in their own community. Unfortunately, in the world of aid, it was not uncommon for Westerners to dictate what type of assistance a foreign community needed without having a full understanding of the culture. Kupenda's aim, however, was not to be paternalistic. Their goal was to offer resources, expertise, and accountability as the Kenyans learned what types of programs worked most effectively within their villages and what they might recreate on their own. The hope was that the Kenyans might gradually assume growing responsibility of the aid being given rather than relying on a seemingly endless supply of foreign cash and aid.

Ultimately it was a strategy that would allow for less dependence and more sustainability.

When Cindy visited Kenya, she was able to offer resources through Kupenda, such as a large supply of hearing aids that were purchased by a founding board member. She was also able to construct two classrooms through the funds given to her by Grace Fellowship Church, which was for the exact amount she needed. At every turn, God seemed to sanction the assistance and love given to the children.

In spite of this, Cindy still struggled with anxiety over how to provide the assistance needed on an ongoing basis. Sometimes the burden left her feeling lonely and inadequate, yet the needs continued to be presented to her. When she returned to the United States she settled back in her home with her Chesapeake retriever puppy, Kambe—similar to Kombe, the surname of her field assistant who protected her in Kenya.

Within a short while, she received e-mails from an assessment officer in Kenya. Her heart sinking, she was informed that Rehema and George's time had run out. Although money had been left with a government assessment center representative, it was not evident that appropriate action had been taken. Not only were these two children the first two deaths in Kenya that Cindy experienced, but the possibility of negligence made her grief that much more acute. The fact that corruption could thwart her well-intended efforts at aid, combined with the level of personal sacrifice she was making for the organization swelled within her and manifested itself on her face in a steady stream of tears.

Shortly after, Andy informed Cindy that he wanted to return to Kenya. Unfortunately, Cindy, working full time at the Army Environmental Center, was unable to get leave to go with him. Resigning herself to being left behind, she encouraged him to go and to keep in touch. When Andy departed and the days ticked by, however, she became increasingly alarmed when she did not hear from him.

CHAPTER 13

POINT BREAK

However long the moon disappears, someday it must shine again.—African Proverb

Kenya, 2004

For days, Andy and his girlfriend e-mailed friends and family back home. When a porter from a nearby resort showed up where they were staying, they were stunned to learn that their families were frantically trying to reach them. As they eventually learned, no one was actually receiving their e-mails because the monkeys had taken down the phone lines, something that was not altogether surprising throughout the area.

Over the last week, Andy had been exhausted and horrified by the conditions of his latest trip. He was trying to navigate a myriad of problems. When he first arrived at the Gede Special School, he discovered that none of the children were wearing the hearing aids Kupenda donated, each worth a couple thousand dollars. As he probed the issue more deeply, he discovered that the climate, humidity, and dust often damaged the electronic devices. Additionally, the children did not understand the value of the hearing aids enough to even bother to change the batteries, nor was there always someone available to train the children to use them. Unfortunately, many of the children in the deaf classes were those who might benefit most from a hearing aid. Being hard of hearing rather than completely deaf, many of the children still retained partial hearing. With the help of a hearing aid, they might be integrated into mainstream classrooms. Hearing aids were also preferable to the cultural remedy of taking the children to traditional healers. The healers repeatedly cut the lingual frenulum, the membrane under the tongue extending to the floor of the mouth. This usually took place when the children were young, but the practice did not produce positive results.

Furthermore, even if the hard-of-hearing students did wear their hearing aids, there weren't any resources for teaching the children how to interpret the sounds around them. If a child already passed their language acquisition phase, it made it that much more difficult to tighten their articulation. Also, many of the teachers did not have adequate training in Kenyan sign language, partly because Kenyan sign language was still in the process of being standardized. Much like American Sign Language, the signs the children learned did not conform to the same grammatical sentence structure as the written word. Since tests were not adapted to accommodate the structure of Kenyan sign language, most deaf students recorded subpar test scores in reading and writing nationwide.

Culturally, many hard-of-hearing children were also at a disadvantage at home. Due to traditional understandings of gender roles, it was not considered appropriate for a parent to speak closely to a child of the opposite sex. Therefore, the child was not able to decipher how a parent's lips were moving to interpret their speech. Additionally, many parents feared that their child might lose or mishandle the expensive hearing aid, often forcing the child to take it out and put it in a safe place. All of these factors ultimately limited their child's communication.

The community at large was also a deterrent to improvement. Anyone wearing a hearing aid was automatically stigmatized. It was just one more thing that contributed to the insularity of the deaf population, making the children feel even more different from those around them.

While visiting the deaf children at the school, Andy felt compassion for the students whose lives were limited, but whose love was not. Whenever he arrived at the school gates, the children ran to greet him and hold his hand. Within minutes of an introduction, they assigned him a sign name. Brushing their fingers across their faces, the children mimicked the creases in his forehead. It seemed that they always chose a sign that represented people's most unique features, likely also their greatest insecurities. Cindy's sign name was a sweep of the hand across the left forearm, indicating the part of her limb that was missing. The motions literally translated to "hurt arm." Other visitors were given sign names according to their features: an unsightly mole, a double chin, or a curvaceous figure. Despite his lack of sign knowledge, Andy was often able to identify who the children were referring to by their obvious gestures.

Some of his best moments in Kenya were when he was spending time with the children, playing soccer in the field, or coming up with games. The children loved to play duck, duck, goose with the deaf students pushing the students with physical impairments around the circle when they were chosen to be "it." An aspiring youth leader at his church back home and a playful personality, Andy naturally meshed with the children. Tall and athletic, he flung the children on his back for piggyback rides and games. In response, the children hungrily consumed the novelty of his kindness and attention as if it was their last meal. For Andy, it was a welcome respite from the other conflicts he encountered.

During their tour of schools in the district, Leonard assessed the children while Andy and his companion helped fill out child sponsorship forms and took measurements of the children for wheelchairs. A donor from home wished to donate as many wheelchairs from the United States as the organization needed. After days of taking notes on approximate sizes, however, they learned that it would cost more to ship the wheelchairs than to simply buy them in Kenya.

Unfortunately, purchasing materials abroad was just not an option for every donor. Some donors did not have the money to purchase the items in Kenya when they already had the materials in the United States. Others wanted to oversee all aspects of the purchase but did not want the challenge of having to do so in Kenya. Still others did not want to support a foreign economy. On the other hand, buying materials locally was an ideal option for the sustainability of the Kenyan market. Foreign donations of clothing, mosquito nets, and other items had a dark history of putting local vendors out of business. The destruction of the small businessman ultimately caused Kenyans to be more dependent on the welfare of others.

Andy also discovered other conflicts when he toured the special-needs classrooms. There he found large crowds of children, sometimes fifty people to a room. This was still an improvement from the one hundred or so children per room found in the mainstream classrooms. Additionally, he and his companion noticed that a wide variety of needs ranging from physical challenges to learning disabilities were lumped in the same group. For instance, one child who operated at a seemingly average level was labeled with a disability and placed in a special classroom rather than being tutored, simply because he was a slow reader.

Between each school visit, Andy, Leonard, and those traveling with them rode in the back of a pickup truck on top of a mattress. Bouncing along the bumpy roads, it was virtually impossible to hold a conversation. That was on the days their transportation even arrived. On some days, their driver, scheduled to show up at nine a.m., didn't arrive until much later. Without any way to communicate with him from the A Rocha guesthouse where they were staying, they were subjected to a cultural notion of time vastly different from their own.

Amid all the tumult, Andy took refuge in Leonard, who had taken vacation time from his job to help with Kupenda-related tasks. Whenever they witnessed something unusual, Leonard was the first to verbalize the sentiment. With few people to trust, they depended on Leonard and his history of reliability, intelligence, and resourcefulness. Just one year earlier, Andy visited Guatemala and questioned whether Kupenda was able to branch out to other countries to offer its services. Unfortunately, without a trusted and committed contact such as Leonard who could navigate the social and cultural waters of the area, they quickly realized that expanding Kupenda was not possible, particularly at this early stage in the organization's development.

When the phone lines were finally restored, Andy reiterated the events of the last few days to his sister, Cindy, who was on a work trip to Hawaii. Alarmed, she knew of no better way to sort through her anxiety than through physical exertion. Since she was in the middle of surfing lessons, she threw herself into them with new vigor. As she did, she was faced with a not-so-subtle metaphor for her life. Exhausting herself by trying to paddle out to the point break and catch a wave, she often found herself pushed backward. Impatient and frustrated, she found herself taking waves before she was ready, causing her to fall and have to paddle all over again. Just like Kupenda, every step forward came with a couple of steps back.

CHAPTER 14

THANKSGIVING

Let the elephant fell the trees, let the bush pig dig the holes, let the mason wasp fill in the walls, let the tall giraffe put up a roof—then we will have a house.—African Proverb

Kenya, July 2004

By the time Cindy returned to Kenya, she tried to manage expectations. Over the past few years, the Kenyans repeatedly requested the services of a speech therapist. With the help of a donation from a friend in her church, Cindy returned to Kenya with her friend Laura, a speech therapist she met while in grad school who was eager to offer assistance. Unfortunately, it seemed that the first order of business was to convince everyone that a speech therapist was not magically able to make children speak. Instead, Laura hosted workshops for the teachers on articulation, language, fluency, and voice. She also showed them how to use a picture-exchange system so nonverbal children were able to point at pictures such as food, a toilet, or a smiley face to express their needs and feelings. Additionally, she was able to tutor the children on how to identify different sounds and on how to read lips. Although it felt as if her contributions were merely scratching the surface of a gaping need, she helped establish a precedent for the teachers to imitate.

Kenya, November 2005

When Cindy visited Kenya again the following November, she began to see more fruits of her labor. Part of these fruits came from her active involvement in the disability ministry at her church, Grace Fellowship Church in Timonium, Maryland. Grace had decided to invest in Cindy's vision by holding a Thanksgiving offering to be given to Kupenda and allowing the organization to host a benefit concert on their premises. With fresh resources, Kupenda was able to sponsor twenty-nine children to attend school, board overnight, and receive three meals a day, as well as hire two teacher aides.

Meanwhile, the compound at the Gede Special School was also expanding. The Rotarians added an office for the head teacher, as well as two classrooms for children with cerebral palsy. Kupenda also provided two additional classrooms for the deaf. The organization additionally partnered with the African Medical and Research Foundation (AMREF) and the children's parents to build an additional boarding facility. The school that started as an idea in Leonard's mind was now flourishing, and the children were proof.

During her first tour of the school five years ago, Cindy met Rashid, a boy with hydrocephalus who attended class in the corner of Leonard's office. Rashid was making marked progress and even began to dream of one day becoming the village chief and living in a nice house. During one of Cindy's visits, he thanked her by diplomatically extending his hand. Other children also began to improve with the help of corrective surgeries supported by the organization and with additional assistance from the Association for the Physically Disabled of Kenya (APDK).

Another part of the trip was spent interviewing the children and trying to gather information for sponsors. As Cindy attempted to standardize a questionnaire to mark progress, she encountered a number of cultural barriers.

Starting with a simple question, she asked, "How is this child doing in school?"

The response she received was less than descriptive. The Kenyans responded, "Fine."

Trying another avenue, Cindy asked, "What is the child's handicap?"

To this the Kenyans responded, "They're physically handicapped."

After discussing for many hours what was needed, Cindy worked with Leonard to create a standard form that all parties understood. The information was then written into reports to be given to sponsors in the United States on an annual basis.

Other cultural barriers included a disparity in methods of thinking. The Kenyan education system was largely based on rote memorization and literalism rather than creativity and problem solving. If you wanted to hire someone to build a wheelchair ramp, the job would be completed in that it allowed a child to move from point A to point B. Unfortunately, the ramp might be built at an extreme angle, which caused the kids to fly down at a breakneck speed. If you wanted a child to get a prosthetic, he or she would be given one; however, it might just be the first one in storage rather than the one that matched the child's skin color. Conversely, the literalism of the Kenyans could also be impressive. Their ability to remember dates and times off the top of their heads spoke to the strength of their oral histories and highlighted the lack of many Americans to adequately listen.

When communicating, both the Kenyans and Americans possessed an array of accents that were stumbling blocks to both parties. The Kenyans frequently switched up the pronouns for "he" and "she," while few Americans bothered to learn a proficient amount of Kiswahili at all. The Kenyans also expressed more emotion than Americans, which could easily translate to overly dramatic or overly distant, depending on the audience.

Other cultural conflicts came from situations that were simply unprecedented. When Cindy was informed that the parent of a child was eaten by a crocodile, she had no frame of reference as to how such an incident was normally handled. Thankfully, Cindy and Leonard held an open line of communication to discuss expectations from both sides of the cultural divide.

Unfortunately, even if communication was going well, the job was arduous. As the days of her trip continued to tick by, Leonard decided that they needed to visit the rural town of Marafa. Traveling by motorbike, the two took a grueling two-hour drive on difficult roads. Along the way, the cars, trucks, and motorbikes elbowed for room in a conversation of honking horns. With little regard for speed limits, they passed one another in a race along gravel roads where only white stones marked the presence of upcoming speed bumps. When the wet season came, so did raindrops like bullets that left crater-like potholes punched into the ground like Morse Code. Although the children sometimes filled the potholes for tips, it was only a matter of time before the weather undid their efforts once again.

Not only were the roads in complete disarray, they were lacking stop lights and road signs. As a result, visitors were advised to use the service of a professional driver. In this case, Leonard steered while Cindy clung to the bike with a tight death grip, her oversized backpack bouncing behind her. With her short stature and large helmet, she had what Andy termed "the Marvin the Martian look." By the time they returned later that day, Cindy felt pummeled by the roads and sun. Despite his aversion to Western food, Leonard accompanied her to a restaurant in town because he observed her weariness. He had never seen her so exhausted. Patiently he waited for her to finish a Coke and a snack.

Overall, Cindy felt overwhelmed. It seemed that the time it took to travel to and from Kenya amounted to more than the time she was able to stay in the country itself. As she tried to keep up her frenetic pace and accomplish all of her goals before returning to work, others began to take notice. Witnessing her anxiety, one of the teachers intervened. Madam Karo invited Cindy to take a break from her activities and join her for a cup of tea. A beautifully poised woman, she was calm and competent. Transferred to the Gede Special School in 2004, she had watched as the school was transformed by Kupenda's help.

Although Cindy did not want to slow down, she learned over time how important it was to take time out to spend with the people. She arrived at the school and entered a classroom where she was taken aback by what she saw. Inside a crowd was gathered around an impressive display of food. As Cindy was ushered to a seat, the teachers and a host of others involved with Kupenda began to speak. The Kenyan community had a great affinity for reciting speeches. One by one they explained the difference Kupenda made in the children's lives. Before the children received Kupenda's expression of love, most of them defined themselves by the undignified circumstances in which they lived. When the children at the Gede Special School were asked what their family did for them during a social studies lesson, they often did not have much to say. Yet when they were asked what Kupenda did for them, they responded with a lengthy list, often culminating with the profound but simple answer: love.

When it was Cindy's turn to speak, she expressed her appreciation, not only because of the outpouring of love but because the Kenyans were not aware that it was Thanksgiving Day. Away from home, she considered those at the school her family. Although her hosts frequently apologized for not being able to reward her efforts more fully, Cindy felt differently, telling them, "I have my reward now. To see a child smiling that used to wince in pain or a student walk that used to be confined to a wheelchair—it's an incredible privilege that God has invited me to be a part of."

She hoped that one day, when the children looked back on their lives, that they would remember a woman from America who thought they were special and gave them an opportunity to become something extraordinary.

Cindy with Madam Karo in 2010.

With all of the praise focused on her, Cindy noticed someone else who needed to be recognized. The cornerstone Kupenda depended on in Kenya was Leonard, who was already taxed to an alarming degree. Both she and Andy decided the only way to ensure sustainability was to hire him full time. Although she had hinted such hopes to Leonard in the past, even visiting him for a week the previous September to discuss job possibilities, nothing was ever made concrete. She had always worried about how to raise a steady source of income in order to ensure his livelihood. In conversations with her family, however, her parents had agreed to financially assist with the salary in the case of an emergency. She also knew her church had pledged their Thanksgiving offering to the organization. With this in mind, Cindy decided to step out of her comfort zone and formally offer Leonard a position as the Kenya director of the organization. In the back of her mind, however, the recognition of the sheer number of families now counting on Kupenda translated to a roll call of pressure.

Meanwhile, Leonard, knowing the future uncertainty of an organization in its infancy, took time to weigh his passion and possibilities against the stability of his family's well-being. The decision to resign from his job at job at KEMRI (the Kenya Medical Research Institute) was like pulling a string in a complex embroidery. He did not know if he was simply fixing a dangling thread or if a substantial part of his life would become unraveled with the pull. In the end, he couldn't deny his desire to be a more active part of the solution to help children with disabilities as opposed to his former work done in research. Therefore, he began his new job as the coordinator of MADISERO, the group of special-needs experts affiliated with Kupenda for the Children, all while knowing that the warmth and security of his life were now at risk.

CHAPTER 15

THE COMMUNITY'S CURSE

Therefore, strengthen your feeble arms and weak knees. "Make level paths for your feet," so that the lame may not be disabled but rather healed.—Hebrews 12:12–13

Kenya, 1971

Yaa Mangi nestled in the treetops outside the school and peered over at the children attending their lessons. He longed to join them and to experience the excitement of learning new things, but his father insisted that his children stay at home to help earn money by making *mnazi,* or wine, derived from the sap of palm trees.

Although the village officials required that at least one child from each family receive an education, his father chose his younger brother over him. When his younger brother did not want to go, the village chief threatened to take his father to court. Finally his father agreed to send Yaa.

At fifteen years old, Yaa joined his friends at the school run by a neighboring church. In Kenya, it was common for schools to be started by missionaries and then sponsored by their churches. During Yaa's time as a student, his favorite activity was listening to the evangelist who visited the school and told Bible stories. Knowing that his family disapproved of Christianity due to their Muslim beliefs, he kept his interest a secret. After a while, he even began attending church on Sundays, telling his parents he was doing extra work at school. On the day that he accepted Christ, he resorted to saying his prayers while everyone else was sleeping.

Over time, however, his new faith became more and more difficult to conceal. When his brother became older and decided to attend the same school, he reported Yaa's new beliefs to his father, but his father simply did not believe it was true.

As Yaa's faith influenced his actions and he no longer smoked or drank, his grandfather asked him, "Is it true that you have been saved?"

Anxious and fearful, Yaa replied, "No!"

Eventually, Yaa shared what he learned about Christ with his mother. Together they prayed secretly. As Yaa grew older, he was finally able to muster enough courage to answer his grandfather's questions truthfully. When he decided to marry, his refusal to take part in aspects of his family's traditions that conflicted with his Christian ones was considered rebellious. His father became irate. Chasing him from their home, he spewed curses at him, telling him he would be childless. At the climax of his rant, he even threatened death.

Despite his father's prophecy, however, Yaa's first son was born a short while later. The event ultimately influenced many of his neighbors to ask the name of his god, which was so much stronger than his father's. He told them: Jesus Christ.

Kenya, 2006

By 2006, Yaa's name was changed to Robert when he was baptized into the Anglican Church. Having attended Bible college, he gained experience working as a clergyman alongside another pastor. Shortly after his ordination, Rev. Mangi was posted in Nairobi, where he worked for two-and–a-half years. Then he transferred to three other churches and worked as the bishop's chaplain. Eventually he was sent to work in coastal towns. In Gede, he started a church through a crusade. Preaching in the streets, he called people to come and learn about the Lord and invited them to attend church in a small structure next to the Gede School.

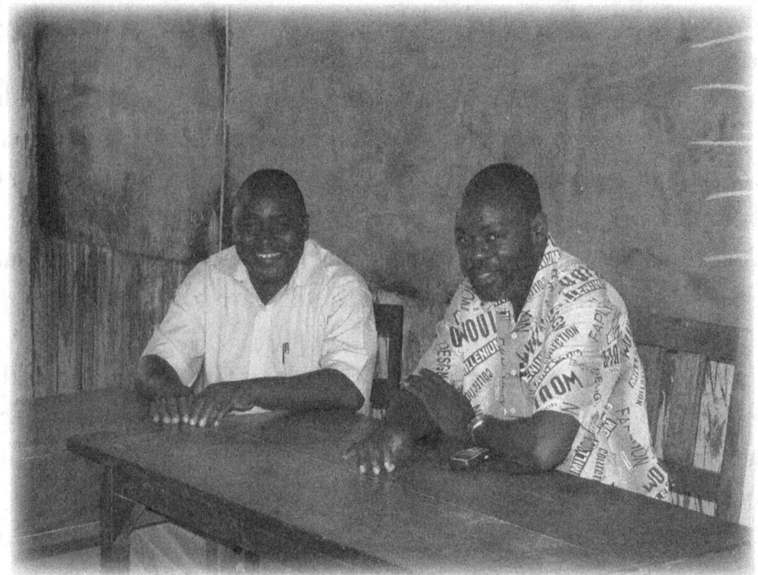

Reverend Mangi with Gabriel, a teacher for the deaf at the Gede Special School, in 2007.

As he began to establish himself, he was invited by Leonard to attend a meeting for community leaders. As he listened, Leonard summarized the community's attitudes toward those with disabilities. Reverend Mangi agreed, the Bible was for all people, yet he rarely saw people with disabilities in church. Part of the problem lay in the deeply entrenched philosophy of the "Prosperity Gospel," or the belief that if you followed God you would be blessed with good things. The influence of the Prosperity Gospel led many to believe that if you suffered, God was punishing you. According to the beliefs of many people in the room, if someone had a disability, he or she probably deserved it. Such views were largely attributed to isolated scriptural passages by pastors who did not have access to comprehensive theological training or were a hybrid of tribal and Christian beliefs.

At Leonard's suggestion, Reverend Mangi agreed to help host a pastor workshop during Cindy's next visit. Cindy brought her uncle Randy, a pastor from a small town in Maine, in hopes of connecting the local church to the work of Kupenda. For Cindy, Kupenda had become a family affair. Her dad helped manage the PO box, and her mom contributed her experience working at H&R Block by helping with bookkeeping. Now her uncle was coming to lead a pastor workshop since the church was one of the main hubs for politics, news, and community impact in Kenya. If other pastors could get onboard about teaching the truth of loving people with disabilities, they had the potential to create significant cultural transformation.

To get things started, Reverend Mangi wrote letters to pastors of all denominations, inviting them to the workshop. When about thirty of them gathered together before Randy, there was an obvious tension in the room. The fact that a mzungu, or white person, was here to tell them what to do created a hostile environment right off the bat. As a result, Randy decided to begin by asking *them* questions. Rather than preaching to them, he listened.

Relieved, the pastors began opening up. One by one they began to share stories of people with disabilities that they knew.

Randy followed up after their stories by asking, "What does Jesus say about how to treat people with disabilities?"

As the pastors looked at passages of Jesus caring for the lame and blind, they began to get excited by the evidence that Jesus loved all people, even those with disabilities.

In John 9, Jesus' disciples came across a man born blind. They asked him, "Rabbi, who sinned, this man or his parents, that he was born blind?"

Jesus responded, "Neither this man nor his parents sinned, but this happened so that the work of God might be displayed in him."

As the participants discussed the scriptural teachings that people with disabilities were not cursed because of sin, they were stunned.

Opening his Bible to Matthew 25, Randy read, "Depart from me, you who are cursed, into the eternal fire prepared for the devil and his angels. For I was hungry and you gave me nothing to eat, I was thirsty and you gave me nothing to drink, I was a stranger and you did not invite me in, I needed clothes and you did not clothe me, I was sick and in prison and you did not look after me.

"The people around him responded, "'Lord, when did we see you hungry or thirsty or a stranger or needing clothes or sick or in prison, and did not help you?'

"He replied, 'Truly I tell you, whatever you did not do for the least of these, you did not do for me.'"

Before a roomful of fellow pastors, Randy asked them, "If we are the ones not doing what God has called us to do, who is really being cursed—those with disabilities or those of us who look the other way?"

Within just one day of the workshop, local churches were beginning to form groups in their congregations to discuss how to make their churches accessible to people with disabilities. Within two days, a girl who was deaf appeared at one of these churches through the help of a pastor from the workshop.

In the months following the workshop, Reverend Mangi began putting even more of Randy's lessons into practice. Working with Leonard, he preached about loving people with disabilities, encouraging his congregation to bring people with disabilities to church. He was surprised to find that the culturally controversial message was well received.

Going even further, he encouraged his congregation to volunteer with the special-needs children at the neighboring Gede Special School and even sponsor a child as a church. Soon, some of the women even began helping to feed the children while others volunteered to take the children to services. The two neighboring structures that were previously separate were slowly becoming knit together.

Yet that was not the only thing remarkable that came from Randy's trip to Kenya. Also joining him were two recent college graduates about to embark on an epic adventure.

CHAPTER 16

LARGER THAN LIFE

If you think you are too small to make a difference, try sleeping in a closed room with a mosquito.—African Proverb

United States, 2006

Pat and Adam agreed to accompany Cindy, Randy, and Andy to Kenya. Their enthusiasm was enough to expand the parameters of almost any room. The two were more like brothers than friends. With messes of blond hair and beards, they looked like lumberjack surfers, and at first glance, it was hard to take them seriously. To anyone who spent time with them, however, they were like a moving train. Either you jumped onboard for the onslaught of coming adventures or you were left in their wake.

Back at home in Maryland, the two lived with a houseful of friends with so many nicknames that it was sometimes hard to keep their stories straight. Successful athletes, they'd competed in a stunning variety of triathlons, Ironman competitions, and running and cycling events.

Pat, twenty-five, and Adam, twenty-four, both had successful careers. However, when they transitioned into their occupations after college, they were unnerved by the pointlessness of their days. While everything was going well on paper, none of it seemed to contribute anything to the world other than to promote their own interests. The two wondered how they might use the things they loved in a way that mattered to more than just themselves. They were already in the beginning stages of fundraising for diabetes research since Adam was a type I diabetic, but they were still looking for a way to contribute something more tangible.

Their solution came shortly after they embraced Christianity when they attended a church retreat. It was there that they listened to Cindy give a compelling talk about Kupenda. It was a lightbulb moment; they both knew this was a cause that would help them find the more meaningful life they both craved. Shortly after introducing themselves, Pat and Adam threw themselves into Cindy's life headfirst. In fact, they became like her rambunctious younger brothers. Within six short months, they were even accompanying her to Kenya. Hoping to get a better idea of the organization's needs, they took a marathon tour of the schools and the children's homes.

Completely unprepared for what they would experience, the two accomplished athletes were exhausted, often forcing themselves to sleep during their long and bumpy car rides. Other times they played with the children at the Gede Special School and showed them how to use a computer. Although the computers never had a terribly long life span due to the climate, the children were still enamored with the PCs and their new larger-than-life heroes.

Pat and Adam also spent a few days doing manual labor. Leonard had recently created a Kupenda office by erecting a partition in a room on the side of his home. Pat and Adam worked with a local man named Nelson on building a ramp to the office. Although Pat and Adam were extremely fit, they were put to shame by their new companion. Despite their best efforts, they watched in amazement as Nelson finished twice the amount of work in half the amount of time.

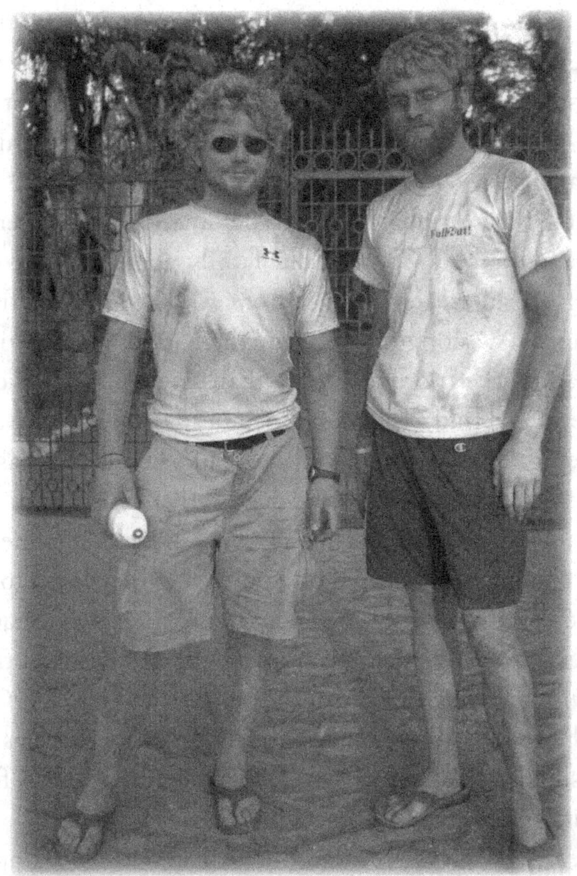

Pat and Adam after a day of labor in Kenya in 2006.

Another part of the trip was spent traveling to Marafa, the very rural and most impoverished region that Kupenda assisted. There they learned that one of the greatest needs of the area was to build a small home, or dormitory, at the mainstream school. Currently, there was nothing being done in this village to assist children with disabilities. It was just too difficult to offer assistance if there was nowhere for children with disabilities to stay near the school.

Since Pat and Adam were always eager to address a new challenge, they started to formulate a plan. In the past, the two had biked from Baltimore to Ocean City, Maryland. Their efforts helped them raise $7,000 for diabetes research. Spurred on by their success, they were already planning to aim even higher. Instead of biking across Maryland, they had been planning to bike across the entire United States while fundraising for diabetes research. After their experiences in Kenya, they knew they also wanted to use their ride to fundraise for Kupenda. To make it even more challenging, they were going to do it on fixed-gear bikes, which did not allow for coasting.

Beginning their campaign back at home, the two friends hosted fundraisers and spoke to friends and family about their cross-country goal. Taking off an entire summer from work with their friend Jesse, they flew out to Washington to begin their journey. In a zigzag route across the nation, the trio biked more than six thousand miles, sleeping wherever they could find a spot to lay their heads. In each state they passed through, they gave talks to schools and clubs about the reason behind their epic trek. Adam's diabetes, the disease that caused him to struggle throughout numerous points of his personal and athletic life, was their compass for compassion. Spurred on to use what they loved to help other diabetics, they were soon inspiring others to use their own unique passions for their relevant greater good. In fact, they even registered their efforts into a formal non-profit called Adventures for the Cure (AFC). For this adventure, they were raising money on a large scale for diabetes research as well as on a smaller, more tangible scale for a boarding facility for children with disabilities in Kenya.

Documenting their expedition, their friend and videographer, Philly K, tagged along in a support vehicle with his brother, Andy. The support vehicle, a 1992 Nissan Sentra dubbed the "AFC mobile," barely survived the trip with its hood held down by a bungee cord. When the entourage wasn't baking in the summer heat, scouring for shelter, battling injuries, or giving talks, they loosened up by singing karaoke in each state—a feat better suited to some of them than others!

By the time they moved through the Appalachian Mountains, the hardest section of their route, they were spent. They pressed on toward their goal, motivated to see friends and family at the finishing line in Ocean City, Maryland. They even pressed forward through gale-force winds and flying debris from tropical storm Ernesto, not letting even the most severe of conditions derail their arrival. Finally passing through the storm and reaching the coast, they found their friends and family eagerly awaiting them. Some of their supporters even rode the last few miles with them.

Patrick Blair, Jesse Stump, and Adam Driscoll of Adventures for the Cure, riding in front of the Grand Tetons during their cross-country trek in 2006.

As a final culmination to their trip, they raised more than $10,000 for diabetes research and $20,000—which, along with $7,000 from friends Glenn and Debra Weinberg, was the requisite amount needed for the Kupenda boarding facility.

Countless sunburns and saddle sores later, the school in Marafa was able to break ground and lay the foundation for the first small home in the area. For one little girl in Marafa named Rehema, who until that time spent her days locked in a hut, the completion of the home could not come soon enough.

CHAPTER 17

A DIFFERENT WAY OF CREATION

Praise be to the God and Father of our Lord, Jesus Christ, the Father of compassion and the God of all comfort, who comforts us in our troubles, so that we can comfort those in any trouble with the comfort we ourselves receive from God.—2 Corinthians 1:3–4

Kenya, 2006

In the summer of 2006, Cindy and Andy returned to Kenya with their first official volunteer team. With nineteen participants, it was an unwieldy task to manage all the trip details. Flying into Nairobi, they rented a *matatu*, or public van, to taxi them to the coast. Unfortunately, the trip that was supposed to take about eight hours ended up taking almost sixteen. Each person brought one suitcase full of personal items and one suitcase full of supplies for the children. The luggage was compressed so tightly on top of the van that it actually shattered one of the windows.

Eventually they reached the tree house where they were staying. Created by an environmental artist, the house rose in tiers from the ground in walls of stucco ornamented with elaborate mosaics and sweeping, open-air windows, topped with thatched roofs. On the second floor, a wooden and rope bridge connected to an adjacent house for additional visitors. Although the woods maintained the structure's rustic quality, it was understandably a vied-for vacation spot.

As they settled in, Cindy felt anxiety and fatigue envelop her. The volunteer trip marked the first time she invited a group of people into one of the most vulnerable areas of her heart—an area with limitless needs that she tried to meet in addition to her full time job. She wondered how they might react to Kupenda and the culture in Kenya. She wondered if they would focus on the lack of furniture in the classrooms or the fact that countless children were now receiving an education. She wondered if they would treat the people with respect or whip out their cameras and snap pictures like visitors in a zoo. She feared they would compare the schools and services only to what was provided in the United States, rather than recognize that assistance for people with disabilities was still developing in Kenya.

Kupenda's goal was to make services for children with disabilities comparable to what was being offered to the general student population. For many of these children, the modest conditions were still a vast improvement from home. Through Kupenda, students were not only receiving an education, they were receiving the kind treatment, food, shelter, medical attention, and personal care that are vital to human dignity.

Although Kupenda was supporting six schools in the area, Cindy decided it was best to have the volunteers go to the Gede Special School, where most of their efforts were focused. For some, their first reactions were what she feared. They focused on the metal bunk beds, limited clothing, and lack of toys. It wasn't until they began going on home visits and watching the children beg to come back to school that they began to see what an improvement the school was for them.

For the duration of the trip, Cindy decided to split the volunteers into two groups. Half assisted teachers in the classrooms, including Leonard's brother, Chengo, who was now a teacher for the deaf. The other half of the volunteers helped start construction on a special-needs classroom, sponsored by Kupenda and the Koinonia Foundation. For the group doing manual labor, they marveled at how challenging it was to break up the rocky soil in order to lay the foundation. After digging in the heat for hours, the mother of one of the students came by to help. Dropping her things, she picked up a shovel and plowed ahead. Before long, one lone woman accomplished more than an entire team of Americans. In fact, her efforts would eventually spur Kupenda to start hosting volunteer days where parents and community leaders could directly serve the school and students.

Not wanting to harm the community by making them dependent on foreign aid, the volunteer days were a great way to get the community vested in being part of the solution to improving the lives of children with disabilities.

Back at the construction site, however, the mother's efforts caused the group to rethink their strategy. One of the volunteers, named Dan, decided to venture out onto the main thoroughfare in front of the school to solicit help. Out of his own pocket, he decided to employ local workers who could complete the task more effectively and efficiently. Within moments it was evident that they were going to see more substantial results.

At the nearby Sir Ali School for the Mentally Handicapped, two other volunteers, Melissa and Kim, worked with teachers from all over the district. The two women were experienced in working with special-needs students and offered to talk with the teachers about autism.

By the second day, one of the teachers raised her hand and asked point blank, "Can we catch disabilities?"

Caught off guard by her question, Melissa took a moment to gather her thoughts. Not realizing the extent of the cultural and educational gap, Melissa explained that it was not possible to "catch" another person's disability.

As she began to listen to the experiences of the teachers, she marveled at the social pressure they faced. For many, their families and friends discouraged their work, telling them they were going to catch the conditions of the children. For Melissa, working in special needs was completely the opposite. When she told people what she did for a living, people often reacted with admiration.

At the end of the day, Melissa opened up about her own background. "I know you know Cindy's story—that she was born without her left forearm," Melissa began. "Many of you look at her as a person with a disability. Yet did any of you know that I had a disability?"

Born with bilateral dislocated hips, she underwent several surgeries as a child. Without this type of medical intervention, she would have been placed in a wheelchair. Breaking cultural modesty guidelines, she hiked up her skirt to show them her scars.

The teachers gasped at her legs in surprise. To them, she seemed to function "normally."

"I know you wouldn't have known I had a disability because I was given opportunities through my school and family. Yet these are opportunities that you can help provide for these children so that their lives do not have to be defined by a physical detail."

Later that week the volunteers were able to show the teachers the potential of people with disabilities on an even greater scale. The group, along with Leonard and staff from the Gede Special School, hosted the very first "Disabilities Awareness Day." Pushing the children in wheelchairs and leading the way, they paraded through the streets of the village, singing and celebrating. The sight of children with disabilities for native Kenyans was alarming enough, never mind the fact that they were trailed by mzungus, or white people.

The first Disabilities Awareness Day
parade in Gede in 2006.

Some of the tourists in the area honked their car horns and threw candy out the window at the children. Angered by their actions, one of the teachers for the deaf asked them to stop. Some tourists were already a source of frustration because of their support of the child sex industry. The teacher did not want to encourage the children to be lured by gifts from tourists or to be treated like animals. Instead, the teacher explained to the tourists that what the children desired more than gifts were edification and understanding.

Afterward, all the villagers were invited back to attend performances and a feast at the school. Sitting at a table reserved for the guests of honor, Cindy looked out at the gathering crowd. More than a thousand faces looked back at her own. It seemed the community had come out in droves, curious to see why people were loudly proclaiming the value of these children. As the schedule of events for the day began, Cindy watched politicians give speeches and the children perform sign language poems, dance, sing songs, and act out short dramas.

Leonard at the Kakuyuni School during Disabilities Awareness Day in 2008.

Children with disabilities demonstrating their skills at the Disabilities Awareness Day at the Sir Ali School in 2011.

In one scene, a tiny little girl tried to resemble Cindy by wearing a blonde wig and carrying a large purse—the only American-looking accessories she was able to find, despite the fact that Cindy is a brunette. The child went through the motions of talking to parents and pretending to bring their children to school. As Cindy watched, she realized that as Kupenda's influence continued to grow, so did people's expectations of her.

In fact, one young man heard about her all the way back in Lamu, a bus ride more than eight hours away. The young man, Anthony, suffered from a condition where his right leg was shorter than his left. Using a crutch to get around, Anthony struggled to fit in among his community. When his mother died and his father remarried, his stepmother treated him harshly, forcing him to do difficult manual labor on their farm. Without the money to finish school, Anthony found it difficult to find employment due to rampant discrimination toward people with disabilities. Desperate, he prayed to God for help. He felt as if he had taken his life as far as he was able to on his own. In timing that Anthony described as "heaven sent," he was soon summoned by his pastor, a friend of Reverend Mangi's, who told him about Kupenda. Traveling to Gede and approaching Cindy and Andy at the Disabilities Awareness Day, Anthony brought a copy of his grades, all straight As, and shared his story. As he talked to them, he began to feel like he belonged for the very first time.

A short while after the volunteers had returned home, they sent word to nineteen-year-old Anthony that they had raised the funds for him to go to Kampala University in Uganda. Overjoyed, he felt a surge of hope and threw himself into his studies. Profoundly grateful for the opportunity, he hoped to use his own disability as a platform to help others. Going through the streets near his school, he sought out children with disabilities, telling them not to give up hope but to keep fighting. Maybe one day they, like him, would receive an opportunity for greater things. Eventually, he formalized his efforts by creating the Kampala University Kupenda for the Children Club. When he tried to get others involved, he was often met with laughter. While only a handful of people were moved by his stories, he refused to let it discourage him.

In the meantime, Kupenda also sent Anthony to Kijabe Hospital in Nairobi to look into the possibility of a prosthetic. Bethany Kids was a program at Kijabe Hospital started by the work of an American doctor named Dick Bransford in 1982. The program included a medical and spiritual ministry to children with disabilities as well as training for medical professionals. Under this program, Anthony learned what would be involved in correcting his disability. After much consideration, however, he decided not to use the money for his leg. Instead, he asked that the organization redirect the funds toward his studies or toward children who needed the same opportunity that he had been given. He no longer considered himself as disabled but as a person "with a different style of walking." In fact, in many ways, he found that his disability was now his strength. For Anthony, Cindy was an inspiration. She was a role model not just because of her disability, but for what she did for others with disabilities.

As he explained, "I tend to think that God created Cindy that way—not disabled, but special and different from others—so that one day she could come to Africa and make the people be treated well and believe in themselves. She helps others believe that they are not disabled but that they are a different way of creation."

By the time Anthony was twenty-six, he would similarly be helping others. Triumphing against older, more seasoned candidates, Anthony was elected a county representative in the Bahari Ward.

As he spoke to the Standard Digital News in Kenya, he elaborated on his views. "I have a dream that one day people with disabilities will live in a nation in which they will never be judged but be loved with what they can accomplish given equal opportunities in the communities they live in."

He summed up with an embellished quote from the movie, *First Knight*: "One thing is certain—God makes us strong so that we serve each other, and in serving each other we become free."

CHAPTER 18

FULLY HUMAN

A family is like a forest: when you are outside it is dense; when you are inside you see that each tree has its place.—African Proverb

Kenya, 2000

One woman who experienced freedom through serving others was a teacher named Victoria. Since 1980, Victoria spent most of her career teaching at the Watamu Primary School. Previously, Victoria had been reluctant to work with children with disabilities since she believed they were a bad omen. She also believed she might be able to catch their disabilities. When Victoria's sister gave birth to a child with cerebral palsy, however, she was forced to rethink everything.

Visiting Leonard at the district's assessment office, she asked him how she might learn more about children with cerebral palsy. Leonard, eager to utilize her new interest, asked her to accompany him on home visits to gather children for the Gede Special School. These experiences gave her a foundational understanding of disabilities. Eventually, Leonard even offered her something more. Job offer in hand, he asked her to help establish the first cerebral palsy classroom at Gede.

As the months ticked by, Victoria found that working with the children was exceptionally challenging. Not only did she provide specialized education, she provided physical assistance as well. Each day she needed to help the children go to the bathroom. Then, when she put an assignment on the board, she needed to help them move their hands in order to write it down. This was all in addition to helping the children actually understand the material she was giving them. Furthermore, the parents seemed to be of little help, often not picking up or returning their child before and after holidays.

On the other hand, she found that this work was surprisingly enjoyable. On days when she arrived in a bad mood, the children welcomed her with an overpowering joy. When she showed patience and kindness, the children responded tenfold. In some cases, the students had limited control over their bodies, but were very mentally acute.

As Victoria described it, "Maybe I was lacking love, but the moment I joined the special section, that love came in. If fifteen years ago I could not handle a kid who was drooling, now I would be happy to work with that child."

In short, her work was a blessing. Honing her skills, she was even given the opportunity to get additional college training. It was upon her return that she found her life remarkably changed.

In 2002, when Victoria returned to the school compound, she took note of many things that were different. In particular, she noticed a new student in the nursery class—an adorable two year old girl named Martha. Investigating her history, Victoria discovered that the girl's parents had abandoned her in the streets of Malindi because she was not able to walk. The lower side of her body was significantly weakened from spina bifida.

Taking note of the tiny child, Victoria was dismayed that Martha did not have anywhere to go during the holidays when school was not in session. Moved by sympathy, she decided to take Martha home to her husband and five children. Her husband, having grown up with the loneliness of being an only child, was only too eager to take her in. Unfortunately, her neighbors were not so gracious. They were confused by her kindness toward someone with a disability and thought her behavior was strange.

In response to their comments, Victoria replied, "Martha needs the same love that my other children need."

As Martha grew older, however, it became increasingly difficult to take her back to school after each holiday.

During many such times, Martha cried and asked her, "Why don't I get to go back home with you each day like your other children?"

Martha grew more and more attached to Victoria's family, and in response, the family opened the fullness of their hearts to her. They began incorporating her into daily life and taking her home at the end of each school day. In the morning when it was time to return, Victoria carried the child on her back to the matatu, the public transportation that took them to the Gede Special School.

For five years, Victoria carried Martha to school and to her therapy sessions with Koffa, the school's occupational therapist. Unfurling the resilient spirit that had lain dormant within, she progressed to the point of using crutches.

When Victoria witnessed her child's progress, she praised the Lord, exclaiming, "We are seeing that God is working wonders through human effort!"

Martha's progression continued until one day she refused assistance altogether. While returning home, she tossed her crutches aside, laboring to put her weight onto one foot and then the other. Her movements had a slow deliberateness to them, yet for each step that remained steady she felt utterly emancipated. To the children from the neighborhood gathering around her, each step was also liberation from their previous judgment of her potential. The same people who once ridiculed her began to clap. They began to see her the way God saw her all along—as fully human and fully worthy of their love.

By 2007, Martha continued to progress, learning to control her movements by consciously pulling her muscles up and in, like shoelaces. Martha explained to Victoria that she was no longer a person with a disability. She wanted to move forward with her life, walking to school on her own and attending mainstream classes. With the joy known only to a mother, Victoria reveled in her adopted daughter's development. She knew there was a purpose for everything that one undergoes on this earth. Fifteen years ago she thought she could not handle a child who was drooling, yet now she found her heart full from the adoption of a child who had a disability. It was as if God was laughing at her earlier misgivings when he introduced her to Martha. When she loved with his love, people were healed.

CHAPTER 19

WAIT FOR YOU

However long the night, the dawn
will break.—African Proverb

Kenya, 2000

Leonard glanced at the ten-year-old girl walking alongside the dirt road. With one leg, she managed to hobble forward with the aid of a crutch, her body rearranging itself with each step like atoms into a molecule. What particularly struck him was that this girl was trying to walk while also carrying a large water container on her head. Piquing his interest, he enquired after her.

When Leonard learned her address, he visited the girl's family at their home. There he discovered that the girl, Teresia, had become injured when she was five while playing soccer. She was running beneath an old mango tree when one of its branches fell on her. Although people came to her rescue, the limb's considerable weight made it virtually impossible to lift. At a loss for what to do, their fear was eventually assuaged when they spotted a passing truck that just happened to be carrying a jack used to lift heavy equipment. With the assistance of the vehicle, Teresia was finally unearthed and carried to a hospital, where she fell into a coma for three long months. When she woke, the doctors said her leg was unsalvageable. The doctors were left with no other choice but to amputate.

By the time Leonard visited her family, he hoped to bring them encouraging news about the Gede Small Home and a possible place for

Teresia there. However, the family focused on their worry about how they would pay for the fees needed to enroll.

In response, Leonard convinced them to take a leap of faith. "Just come," he said. "Maybe something will happen."

In due course, the teachers at the Gede Special School solicited fees from the community to provide food and school fees. Teresia was officially a student.

* * *

In 2000, when Cindy came to visit the Gede Special School for the first time, she took Teresia's picture under a coconut tree. The American was smitten with the girl with the large smile. To others in her community, however, Teresia's disability was a novelty that didn't garner the same endearments. When she walked along the road, she felt the eyes of others circle her like flies. As she struggled to walk, hold her books, or bring water to her home, nobody offered to assist her. Instead, other villagers regularly told her through words and actions that she was useless. They even asked her mother why she bothered to educate a child with a disability.

Complicating her already-troubled existence, one day Teresia's mother delivered a note to her at school telling Teresia that she and her father were getting a divorce. Teresia chose to live with her father for a little while as he had taken over the payment of her school fees, but eventually even this assistance fell by the wayside. This, combined with her mother's poor health, caused Teresia to return to live with her mother and other siblings. Devastated, Teresia wondered how she might finish her education with no resources for school fees, along with the burden of caring for her family. Life was hard enough for a woman in Kenya, let alone one with a disability. Teresia knew life would be even harder if she did not receive an education.

As Teresia walked about doing her chores, her leg began to ache. Although she used a prosthetic throughout primary school, it no longer fit. She also found it cumbersome, as if she was walking with the deliberation of an elephant. Furthermore, the apparatus did not allow for ventilation and ultimately caused her skin to blister. If she wore the device one day, she would need to rest the next. Sometimes the festering wounds stopped her from walking altogether. As others became impatient for her to go faster,

Teresia learned to adapt her routine. She left herself plenty of time so that she would always get to her destination early.

Without prospects for her future, the normally chatty girl became contemplative and withdrawn, her day-to-day life dulled. Observing this, her mother tried to encourage her. She told Teresia to play at the church compound rather than spend time alone in their home. It was one of the few places she found hope.

On Sundays, she sat in the front row of her church class where her teacher pointed out Bible stories about people with disabilities, telling the children that it was wrong to treat any person poorly. When the other children stared at her, her teacher instructed her to sit in the back of the room and stare at them instead.

At home Teresia and her mother prayed together each night. Her mother, who always carried a Bible, reassured her God allowed this to happen for a reason. He allowed her to be different.

"There will be a day when God answers your prayer," she encouraged.

Teresia adopted Psalm 25:21 as her mantra: "May integrity and uprightness protect me, because my hope, Lord, is in you."

She fought to keep her fear at bay but eventually developed ulcers. One day while coming out of church, she found Leonard waiting for her. As she listened to his news, she learned that Kupenda had found someone to sponsor her education. Her prayers were answered!

Overjoyed, she burst into laughter. She felt like Elizabeth in the Bible, who was told that she was finally going to have a child in her old age. Not knowing what to do with herself, she threw her crutches into the air with a sheer pleasure her body could not contain. With her joy taking over new real estate in her life, she turned to Leonard and asked, "When do I begin?"

CHAPTER 20

HAKUNA MATATA

You have hidden these things from the wise and learned, and revealed them to little children."—Matthew 11:25

Kenya, February 2007

The man nervously glanced around the room searching for clues. Interviewing for the position of Leonard's secretary, he sat before a panel of people, trying his best to answer their questions. Leonard had asked him to identify one type of disability. While scanning the panelists, the applicant's eyes landed on Cindy.

"Missing one arm?" he asked, his uncertainty evident by his less-than-confident reply.

Amused, Cindy was reassured that at least one of the applicants was able to answer the question. Many of the others responded by rephrasing the question. When Leonard asked, "What is one type of disability?" they simply responded, "A handicap."

After interviewing a number of unpromising candidates, the group was relieved when they encountered a responsible young man who was professionally dressed. The applicant with the slight stature that made him appear half his age was named Thomas. He responded to their questions articulately, maintained a calm demeanor, and was eager to support Kupenda's mission. He easily surpassed every other candidate for the job.

Satisfied to have completed one more task on her to-do list, Cindy, along with her brother, Andy, moved on to recording a short video for Kupenda and preparing for an upcoming volunteer trip. They also met with the new teacher's aide, named Oripa, at the Sir Ali School. The aide worked with the deaf and those with intellectual disabilities and had volunteered to become the sports director. Her efforts even helped the children go to the Special Olympics when they were hosted in China. She was incredibly dedicated to her job and was an asset to the organization.

Also during their visit, Cindy and Andy checked up on the construction of the new boarding facility in Marafa. There they discovered that five deaf children were holding class under a tree since it was the only place for them to meet. To date, officials counted at least fifty children who were in need of staying at the future facility.

One child who needed to board was a girl named Rehema. Struggling with cerebral palsy, Rehema was forced to stay home while her mother went to the market. She was locked in their hut to protect her from sexual predators who had victimized her in the past. Unfortunately, this was not uncommon for children with disabilities. According to the UN Secretary General's Report on Violence against Disabled Children, children with special needs were particularly at risk for such types of abuse. The report estimated that 90 percent of individuals with intellectual impairments experienced sexual abuse, as well as 80 percent of those who were deaf.

As a result, the girl was suspicious of all visitors. When Cindy and Andy returned with volunteers that summer, her shy nature was immediately evident. She walked with an irregular gait, tucking her arms into her chest and avoiding eye contact altogether. Not only was it intimidating for her to meet strangers, it was a novelty for her to be around mzungus, or white people. Cindy had experienced this during past home visits when some of the children tried to rub her skin to see if the white color would come off.

The group of volunteers talked to Rehema's mother to try to convince her to take her daughter to the new boarding facility. With construction finally completed, the volunteer team, including Pat and Adam, who returned for the official opening, was holding another one of Kupenda's Disabilities Awareness Days in the village. Along with the teacher for the deaf, Mr. Katore, they sought out children rumored to have disabilities. Talking to their guardians, they pled with the parents to bring their children with disabilities out into the open as a public testament to their existence.

For the first time in the town's history, the volunteers and children paraded openly visible through the streets while singing. Since Rehema was not able to walk the long distances on her own, Pat and Adam took turns cradling her in their arms as they walked through the streets. The villagers who gathered at the central market were enthralled by the festivities and eagerly accepted the invitation back to the school.

After many speeches, Pat and Adam cut the ribbon to the front door of the boarding facility amid great fanfare. The boarding facility was just one of the ways their efforts through Adventures for the Cure would grow into a dominant source of support for Kupenda.

After the ceremony, the people were invited to watch other Kupenda-supported children showcase their talents. The students from Gede came and performed a variety of poems, dances, and skits. In fact, their drama had even earned them awards and recognition nationwide. Interspersed with the demonstrations were more speeches and a time for food. The people sat in small huddles, dipping their hands into the communal bowls of beef, rice, and beans.

When they returned to Gede, the volunteer group continued to help by teaching in the classrooms, providing maintenance, and assisting with physical therapy. Some of the volunteers even visited a new autism center to offer their expertise. Together with the children, they learned to sign and sing a song about Kupenda. The Swahili roughly translated to: "Love these children in Jesus' love. Care for and feed them all the days of their life. It is God's kingdom." The music and lyrics were written by Andy while the Swahili portion was written by Chris Magero, who worked for a local hotel's charity services. Ultimately the song was recorded with Andy playing guitar, Cindy leading vocals, and Reverend Mangi and his choir joining in.

In the evening, the volunteers hooked up a projector to Cindy's laptop and showcased *The Lion King.* The images flickered against the wall of the children's dormitory under a vast canopy of stars. Even Leonard's youngest, Esther and Sarah, enthusiastically joined the other children. For many of the students, it was the first time they had experienced a movie. In utter joy, some of the deaf students released their voices, unharnessed, in gleeful abandon. Although many of the children were too young to understand the English being spoken, they still enjoyed the pictures and the occasional Swahili words. They particularly loved the song "Hakuna Matata," translating to "There are no worries!" Snuggling into the volunteers' laps, the children sleepily enjoyed the story unfolding before them.

Other highlights of the trip included numerous budding romances. Pat was in Kenya preparing to propose to his girlfriend and future Kupenda chairperson, Lauren, while Adam was just beginning to date another Kupenda volunteer, named Tracy, whom he would also eventually marry. Cindy's brother, Andy, also began to date his future wife, a Kupenda volunteer named Kate. Kate had lived in Kenya as a child and gone on to assist with various aspects of Kupenda's child sponsorship program and volunteer trips. Meanwhile, Cindy's little sister, Julie, always called J-Bird by her family and friends, and her boyfriend, Jake, also visited Kenya together. Both Julie and Jake helped develop a website for the organization and a database for sponsored children. Their visit was also monumental for other reasons. It was during one evening on the beach where they were staying that Jake proposed to Julie and she accepted. Kupenda seemed to be a connecting force of love for many of the people involved.

By the time the volunteers left Kenya, they felt fulfilled and exhausted. While work on the ground in Kenya continued, including the renovation of a dining hall and kitchen for the children, in the United States a documentary, narrated by Greg LeMond, was being released about Pat and Adam's cycling adventure. Within days of its premiere, Pat and Lauren were married. Touched by their experience in Kenya, they decided to forego a traditional wedding registry and have friends and family donate to Kupenda instead of giving them gifts. Their hope was that this method of giving might serve as a model for couples who wanted to celebrate their own love by sharing with others.

Over the next several years, as Pat and Lauren continued to return to Kenya, they experienced the privilege of watching children walking and gaining independence through the physical therapist their wedding sponsored. The memories became a gift that meant far more to them than any potholder, decorative pillow, or other item they might have received. In fact, while in the eyes of many family members and friends they had "sacrificed," Pat and Lauren felt as if they ended up receiving even more than the students. The relationship with the children was made even more meaningful as they went on to struggle with multiple miscarriages and a failed adoption. It was as if God sowed their tears and created blessings for a community of children half a world away.

One day, however, with a sadness that had become all too familiar, they learned that one of the Kupenda-sponsored children died much too soon. They received word that Rehema, the girl Pat and Adam carried during the last Disabilities Awareness Day Parade, passed away inexplicably before arriving at the boarding facility. Despite investigations, the organization was not able to determine her cause of death. Even more unfortunate, it would not be the only piece of alarming news they would receive.

CHAPTER 21

UNREST

Even if you watch them carefully, small boys can disappear like smoke.—African Proverb

Kenya, January 2008

Cindy was halfway to Kenya when she learned that most of the volunteers were no longer coming. As breaking news headlines described unrest in the area, they started to decline one by one. Only her aunt and uncle were sticking things out, promising to join her shortly. Feeling more vulnerable than ever, Cindy met Leonard at the airport as he filled her in on the latest news.

Within minutes of announcing the results of the Kenyan presidential election on December 30, the incumbent president, Mwai Kibaki, was sworn into office while opposition leader, Raila Odinga, also declared that he was victorious. The situation was further aggravated by tribal tensions and the electoral commission reporting suspicious ballots and manipulated votes. Mayhem ensued in many parts of the country with the Central and Rift Valley provinces experiencing the brunt. When all was said and done, more than a thousand Kenyans were killed, hundreds of thousands were left homeless, and the tourist economy began to plummet. Some of the vendor kiosks in Gede were burned simply because they were owned by certain tribes. The once exemplary African democracy was now in crisis mode.

As the government began banning any type of public gathering, Cindy and Leonard were no longer able to hold meetings at the school. Instead, they visited children at their homes while her uncle held another workshop for pastors. Eventually, however, as violence continued to escalate, Leonard encouraged Cindy, along with her aunt and uncle, to return home a couple of days early.

Cindy returned to Massachusetts where she now lived and resumed her position as an environmental consultant, while occasionally leading whale-watching tours as she had done since 2001. She was also busy corresponding with a fellow researcher of the golden-rumped elephant shrew, an occupational rarity in and of itself. The two shared a deeply rooted interest in wildlife and a commitment to the Lord that naturally progressed into a more serious relationship.

All the while she continued to receive updates from Leonard. Working with Reverend Mangi, they planned a day of prayer and fasting on February 28. Within twenty-four hours the violence had ended. With help from the international community, the two candidates reached a power-sharing agreement that allowed for Kibaki to become president while Odinga took over the newly created post of prime minister. The somewhat-tense arrangement successfully established peace in the nation, but many wondered whether the conflict remained a ticking time bomb until the next election five years later.

In the meantime, teachers and staff tried to pick up the pieces and organize the children back at school. They experienced many setbacks to their schedules and a temporarily limited school menu caused by food shortages. In Marafa, the children slept on hard floors until their order of beds could be delivered to their dormitory along with mosquito nets.

As schools once again reopened, one of the students, Charo Shida, met his friend at the trading post while he was purchasing school supplies. Together they decided to go and watch a game being hosted at the nearby Kakuyuni School before heading back. On their way back, however, Charo Shida became separated from his friend. Since he was unfamiliar with the route, he ended up wandering into the woods. Immersing himself deeper and deeper into the Arabuko Sokoke Forest, he realized he was no longer able to find his way out. For two nights he struggled to survive among snakes and other wild animals, stuffing his fear deep inside the smallness of his body like a parachute in its pack.

Cindy's old field guide, Willy, was giving a tour of the forest to his newest clients when he discovered something rustling in the bushes. As he fought through the bramble, he was stunned to find a little boy in a Gede School uniform. He recognized the boy from when he had accompanied Cindy on a home visit. Although Willy did not know sign language, he was able to piece together bits of the boy's tale, noting a repeated gesture that looked like it referred to elephants. Taking him to his vehicle, he gave him all of the water bottles in the car, along with some bread. Willy found it nothing short of miraculous that Charo Shida had survived the vast threats of the 250 square miles of untamed wilderness. The odds of him surviving as long as he did, let alone being found or being found by someone who recognized him, were scant to none. Surely the Lord was watching over this child!

With the children back in school, the teachers struggled with additional impediments. A newly admitted student named Mohammed Maitha cried constantly. While the teachers initially wrote off his behavior to the change in environment from home to school, eventually one of the house mothers noticed that he was developing a fever. The head teacher, Madam Karo, asked for the house mother to take the child to the hospital.

After receiving care, the child was sent back to the school, where his cries were heard throughout the night, pulling at the heart strings of all the staff. Taking shifts, the house mothers and teachers took turns holding him to make him more comfortable. When his cries finally subsided, they put him to bed until morning, when they discovered he had passed away. Devastated, Madam Karo went to the local hospital where she learned that Mohammed had been discharged prematurely with malaria, a treatable disease.

Unfortunately, the care in public hospitals was frequently unreliable. The Malindi District Hospital served approximately two hundred thousand people in the area with only four ambulances and room for a meager one hundred patients. People lined up for its services but were often sent away when equipment like X-ray machines were not working properly. In the pediatric unit there were twelve nurses, but often only one was on duty at a time. Furthermore, the room itself was overcrowded and stifling, the beds usually housing more than one child at a time. To make matters worse, the room lacked any air conditioning or circulation.

The only other options for health care were the private hospitals, which were often funded by faith-based organizations. With limited space, the rooms boasted openings for a scant ten or eleven children at a time but included air conditioning, separate bathrooms, and beds for relatives. Unfortunately, most of the children's families were not able to afford its use. For the children in Marafa, they did not even have the option of a public or private hospital. The only care in town was provided by a small clinic.

While Leonard attempted to do everything in his power to assist the children with outside resources, Kupenda was still too small to surmount the inadequacy of the country's health-care system. While at times the hospital waived fees due to extreme poverty, Leonard also asked parents to take ownership of a portion of the costs. He also attempted to sensitize local businessmen to the challenges faced by the students by offering school tours that helped them see the needs of children with disabilities. During one such tour, local businessmen decided to finance a feeding program for the children who did not board but still needed adequate nutrition. In addition, a former volunteer gathered funds to provide a nurse at the school and around-the-clock care.

Even with such encouragement, Leonard and other staff still encountered problems, particularly when it came to the parents of the children. For instance, a child named Baraka Kazungu suffered from hydrocephalus. When his mother carried him into the Gede Special School, he was able to receive therapy that allowed him to walk and even feed himself. Unfortunately, all of this progress was undone while he was at home during a school break. He developed a fever and seizures when his parents neglected to administer his medicine, a decision that ultimately contributed to his death.

At his funeral, Leonard proclaimed, "God gave us Baraka to care for, though for a short time. While we loved him, God loved him most."

In response, the staff began doing more community advocacy than ever. A group called the African Leadership and Reconciliation Ministry (ALARM) visited Kenya through the contact of a mutual friend with Cindy. The director of leadership development and his wife spoke to pastors in the area about disabilities. Additionally, their son with Down syndrome was also able to talk about his experience with having a disability to local pastors and to those in attendance at the annual Disabilities Awareness Day.

The staff also began formulating a plan to implement parent meetings. They taught parents about their responsibilities in caring for their children. Cindy and Andy also suggested holding sign language workshops to instruct the teachers and parents of children with hearing impairments how to communicate more proficiently. As Madam Karo pointed out, if the American volunteers were able to visit for two weeks and leave communicating with the children, then it was possible for the parents, too. As it stood, the children often felt more loved by Cindy than their own parents.

In an effort to motivate parents to give greater support to their children, Madam Karo stated, "To the children, Cindy is more of a parent than the real parents. Kupenda has brought hope to the hopeless, love to those who never knew love, a home to the homeless, food to the hungry, light to the darkness, and happiness and laughter to the neglected."

The workshops were one tool for parents and teachers to show the children this same love. For one parent in the audience, this would be illustrated to an astonishing degree.

CHAPTER 22

AMBASSADORS OF LOVE

A friend is someone you can share the path with.—African Proverb

Kenya, 2008

Amani followed Baraka, his curiosity getting the better of him. At fourteen, Amani was unable to attend school. His parents did not see the point because he was deaf. He watched in awe as he saw Baraka, a deaf child just a few years younger than himself, going to the trading post and picking out school supplies. Going out of his way to befriend him, he followed Baraka home. When it was time for Baraka's father, George, to take his son to school, Amani followed them yet again. After George left Baraka at the special school, he found Amani waiting for him. With tears in his eyes, Amani looked up at George, asking through gestures why Baraka was allowed to go to school but he wasn't.

Compelled by the similarity of the boy's circumstance to that of his son, George asked for the assistance of the village chief. Together they visited Amani's parents. It was not long before they expressed their attitudes about their son's disability being starkly negative. Observing the cruelty Amani faced from his parents, George was not able to leave the child with them in good conscience. Since Amani's parents were more than eager to be rid of their burden, George took the child into his home.

Since the birth of his own son, George had learned about the trials of caring for a child with a disability. Due to a complication in his wife's pregnancy, his son had been born with an infection and almost died. When he recovered, he had lost his hearing. They took him to a local witch doctor twice for tongue cutting, a traditional healing method, to no avail. Meanwhile, his neighbors scorned him and told him that his son's condition was a curse from God. They insisted that such a child was unworthy of his care. For George, every experience of his son was one he considered a blessing. He knew in his heart that if he loved this child, God loved Baraka that much more.

Hearing of Leonard's work in the community, George sought him out in his office. With Kupenda's help, his son was able to receive access to an education, as well as resources to pay for boarding fees. As Baraka progressed in his studies and earned good marks in school, his community began to take notice. Time and time again their neighbors expressed their surprise that someone who was unable to speak was able to be educated. If his son was able to be successful, the same might be said for Amani. Allowing Amani to stay at their home, he gave the boy one of his son's school uniforms and helped him enroll through a Kupenda sponsorship. The parents watched as the two boys interacted, delighted that they could communicate with each other in such a special way.

As a testament to his gratitude for God's provision in their lives, George hoped to bring the same type of blessing to others. Since he was retired, he decided to spend every other week making it his personal mission to seek out other children in need of hope. Going door to door throughout the district, he educated the parents, telling them to take their children with disabilities to school. Even though the community at large mocked how he chose to use his time, he did not let it break his will or his motivation. In time, he became a resource for parents and even helped raise money for a Parent Teacher Association.

In recognition of his services to the community, Kupenda saved up to buy him a bicycle. With utter joy, he realized that he no longer needed to walk the long miles between homes while searching for children with disabilities. The organization also recognized him with a "Parent of the Year" award. In front of the other parents of the students gathered at the school, he smiled as he reflected on his situation. The very disability that brought his family scorn now brought him recognition and gifts. It simply confirmed that everything was a gift from God.

* * *

Yet another celebration occurred as Teresia left for college. The same girl who threw her crutches with joy upon learning that Kupenda was able to sponsor her to return to school was now the first Kupenda-sponsored child to finish secondary school. This was an incredible achievement in an area where only 2 percent of kids, including those without disabilities, ever make it to high school (although by 2012, The Education Bill in Kenya would make learning compulsory, penalizing parents who failed to take their children to nursery and secondary school). As if this gift was still too small for God, she was once again overjoyed when her sponsor offered to continue his support of her through college. Studying community development and social work at the African Institute of Research and Development Studies in Eldoret, Teresia was able to utilize the pain of her own experience to help others. She also set to work interning at Leonard's office during her breaks.

Leonard now led a non-governmental organization (NGO) in Kenya called "Kuhenza for the Children." This new entity was derived from the community-based organization called MADISERO, but it was now eligible for more money and partnerships countrywide. The name "Kuhenza" was a local Giriama dialect for "Kupenda." The new title distinguished the Kenyan counterpart from its US-registered sister organization "Kupenda for the Children."

Through her work with Kuhenza, Teresia began helping out by making home visits and talking to parents of children with disabilities. The extra set of hands was useful as Leonard struggled with health challenges related to the onset of ulcers. Yet another one of Teresia's tasks was to talk at *barazas,* or chief meetings, throughout the Malindi District.

Although Teresia often appeared shy and soft spoken at first glance, she knew that one of her greatest assets was her ability to take people to task. The result often left her visitor with the impression that she was both kind and competent. Having lived as a person with a disability, she felt confident speaking with the children's voice.

In one instance, where parents were not taking their child to school, Teresia reprimanded them without hesitation. "Is Leonard supposed to be his parent?" she asked coolly.

During another home visit, she discovered a little boy named Jimmy Katana. The child suffered with ailments to his eyes and ears caused by malnutrition. His parents believed that a balanced diet was too expensive. In response, Teresia set to work. One by one, she began to show them how to use the resources around them to drastically improve the quality of their child's life. She explained about the vitamins their child might receive from nearby mangoes and the rich nutrients from milking their goats. With simple instruction, they were equipped to utilize their own environment for good.

Teresia feeding a child at the Gede Special School in 2012.

At the meetings she organized, she confidently proclaimed, "Disability is not the end of life!"

She was the incarnation of the truth of John 9:3 where a disability is identified as an opportunity for the work of God to be illustrated. The scripture stated that "This [disability] happened so that the work of God might be displayed in him." Deep in her soul, she felt compelled to stand for those unable to stand, walk for those unable to walk, and speak for those unable to speak. She knew that if society understood people with disabilities, it might also organize itself to give everyone more successful lives. She also passionately believed in Mark 9:37, which stated, "Whoever welcomes one of these little children in my name welcomes me."

When Cindy came to visit, the two spent time talking with one another about the self-consciousness that often accompanied their disabilities. When Teresia felt hopeless after other girls taunted her that she would never marry, Cindy told her otherwise, with the caveat that she must finish her education first.

Teresia stayed in school and directed her love toward caring for the children. She dreamt of making a difference in the environment that once rejected her and of finally being fully loved. It was a sentiment Cindy could relate to. She longed for the personal comfort of a partner and ally in her mission. By September of 2008, she began to feel that her longing was being answered. Her relationship with her fellow researcher had grown significantly, culminating in an engagement and an eagerness for the path ahead.

CHAPTER 23

SMALL BEGINNINGS

Who dares despise the day of small things.—Zechariah 4:10

Kenya, 2005

Gabriel sat at his desk reading the newspaper as the boy cried in front of him. For thirty minutes Mabruk cried until his uncle attempted to intervene. Gabriel quickly motioned the uncle away and shook his head. When the boy's sounds subsided, Gabriel folded his newspaper and looked at him.

"Are you through?" he asked.

Mabruk, who was deaf, nodded sullenly.

"Why were you crying?" Gabriel asked. "Don't you like school?"

Mabruk again nodded yes.

"If you are crying, perhaps you want to be sent back to live with your uncle," Gabriel said.

The child's uncle intervened, "If you do not want to be in school, then you will be sent back to your mother in Nairobi. I do not want someone staying with me who does not value his education."

Gabriel looked at Mabruk, silently pondering his fate. The child was first brought to the school when he was very young. Even at that time he held a reputation for being truant. Eventually, however, he went to live with his mother in Nairobi until he was sent back after being kicked out of school for using drugs. Returning to Gede, the family found it difficult to enroll him in school. The head teacher refused to readmit him on two occasions.

When the child showed up a third time with his uncle, Gabriel spoke up. "Let us try to help the child," he said. "If we are going to be defeated, it will be out of our control, but we can try."

Gabriel had a history of defending the children who slipped through the cracks. In the past, he had helped admit a student in order to rescue her from an early marriage, a fate not uncommon in Kenya.

In this case, Mabruk was readmitted to the school where he joined class four. Unfortunately, it was only a matter of days before the boy decided he did not like the rules and restrictions. Soon he began hopping the fence and running away to hang out with the boys on the street. Gabriel often took him aside, reading to him from the Bible. He was at his wit's end and did not know what else to do.

After Mabruk's latest infraction, both the boy and his uncle ended up in Gabriel's office.

Looking at Mabruk's face, full of emotion, Gabriel spoke to him. "Your uncle is now denying you because you don't want to stay in school."

Watching the theatrics ebb away, he saw Mabruk consider his next course of action. After a long while, he responded through sign language.

"I have changed my mind. I will be in school, and I will not give you any problems. I will not run away, and I will only leave when I am given permission."

Despite his skepticism at the boy's proclamation, Gabriel allowed him to stay. By 2008, he began to witness a transformation in Mabruk's behavior. His grades and conduct improved. He was even elevated to the position of head prefect at the school and took the leading role in school plays.

Mabruk at the Gede Special School in 2007.

Mabruk also began expressing interest in learning more about the Bible. He often came to pray with Pastor Brown, a pastor for the deaf, or Reverend Mangi. He also attended church and even began signing short sermons for the other students.

As word got back to Mabruk's father, however, his parents were decidedly less enthusiastic about the change. As Muslims, they blamed Reverend Mangi and Pastor Brown for influencing their son. Under customary Kenyan law, the father maintained the right to choose what religion his children followed. Approaching Reverend Mangi, the father asked him if he was responsible for converting his son to Christianity. Reverend Mangi calmly answered his questions and discussed the matter openly with him. He tried to explain that Mabruk was seventeen years old and made his own decisions. As a result, he encouraged the father to ask Mabruk himself what he preferred. Since his father had not bothered to learn sign language, he used the assistance of an interpreter.

As the father turned to his son, he asked him sharply, "Do you still want to be a Muslim?"

Mabruk responded by looking directly in his eyes and signing, "I would rather slit my throat than become a Muslim."

The father exploded in fury and began to lodge complaints. He spoke to the teachers and housemothers, asking them not to let his son participate in Christian prayers. The school's policy, however, was that both Muslims and Christians participate in classes specific to their religious affiliation, but so far only the area's Christian religion teachers knew sign language.

With a new zeal for the Lord, Mabruk decided he wanted to become a pastor himself one day. At the school he continued to take other children under his wing and amaze the teachers with the new temper of his lifestyle.

Mabruk's life was not the only one that was marked by spiritual transformation. The family of a child named Nassir collectively decided to convert to Christianity. Although they were previously Muslims, they felt transformed by the love they received from Kupenda. Unlike many other organizations, Kupenda followed the biblical mandate to love all children. This was regardless of their religious affiliation and without conditions for conversion. As a result of this openness and care, Nassir's physical hope ultimately led his family to an eternal one.

Unfortunately, not all experiences with religion were as beneficial. There was a sizeable population of people in the area who maintained radical beliefs about healings. In 2009, these beliefs influenced a Kupenda employee named Winnie Gona who worked as a teacher's aide in the cerebral palsy classroom. Winnie, who suffered from AIDS, was often visited by a local pastor who believed she did not need to take her medication if she truly trusted in the Lord's power to heal. As Winnie heeded his advice and refrained from her regimen, her health began to deteriorate. In a short time, Winnie passed away from complications arising from AIDS and TB, leaving her sister to care for her children. Although Kupenda paid for funeral expenses and reached out to the family, the entire organization was affected by the tragic loss.

Sadly, this was not a one-time occurrence. Kupenda continued to witness the damaging effects of superstition. When something negative happened, it was not unheard of for villagers to believe someone had cursed them. Often the elderly were accused and driven out of the village or even killed. Albinos were sometimes killed and their organs harvested due to a belief that they brought prosperity. As neighbor was pitted against neighbor, it became evident that pastor workshops and community education were needed more than ever.

With each overwhelming challenge, however, God seemed to send resources of hope to encourage his love and care throughout the community. Through the grassroots efforts of volunteers and contributors, Kupenda was able to provide emergency medical care, clean water, dormitory expansion, and research into the care of those with disabilities. One particularly strategic donation was made by a volunteer from the United Kingdom named Clare, who helped collect and deliver occupational therapy (OT) equipment to Kenya. After numerous challenges with shipping, the equipment finally arrived to a cheering crowd of teachers and children. Just a couple of years later, Clare would also raise funds to expand the OT room at the Gede Special School.

The problems she originally encountered with shipping were not uncommon to Kenya. Many sponsors of children Kupenda supported wished to send gifts. Unfortunately, the customs and duty costs often ended up exceeding the original value. Not to mention the fact that there was always a high risk of theft or loss once the package was en route. Even if people sent their gifts with Cindy personally, it was often confusing for the children to understand why one child would receive a gift and the others didn't. In order to simplify things, Cindy created a gift fund, providing for such items as toiletries, school supplies, school uniforms, shoes, and other small miscellaneous items. Not only did this help support the local Kenyan economy by buying materials in Kenya, it helped make sure children were being given gifts according to their greatest need. As much as she loved for sponsors to have a more personal relationship with their sponsored children, this method was more effective in keeping administrative costs down and preventing misunderstandings.

Another benefit for the children was the 2009 National Special Needs Education Policy Framework created by the Kenyan Ministry of Education.

The policy proclaimed that discrimination against people with disabilities of any kind was illegal and that children with disabilities were entitled to an education as well as the right to participate in a mainstream classroom if possible. By providing a legal framework for inclusive education, Kenya was once again showing its commitment to empowering citizens with disabilities while also acting as a model for other African countries and the world at large.

At the same time, Kupenda was also able to assist children with disabilities younger than five, who were not yet of school age. The early intervention began to mitigate the effects of disability before they progressed. For approximately $13 per month, the organization offered a feeding program for families of children with disabilities. Each effort of the organization was supported by a handful of volunteers, a church, or a curious tourist.

As a gauge on Kupenda's effectiveness in the community, a Duke University student named Alanna Ahlers would spend a summer in the coastal district of Malindi, surveying how the attitudes of parents of children with disabilities had changed since they received assistance from the organization. It became evident that most of the parents had changed their opinions for the better, but that they continued to struggle with negative attitudes and pressures from their surrounding community.

Alanna would summarize one of her recurrent findings in the following way: "All societal stigmatizations aside, many parents simply cannot afford the care that a child with disabilities needs, and that child becomes a drain on their already limited resources … Then, when the family also faces negative comments, whispers of witchcraft or evil deeds from the community, and their religious community turns a blind eye to their need, it is no wonder that parents are bitter and have not accepted their children. On top of it all, many parents are uneducated, and they have no idea what caused their child's disability, what can be done about it, or how to face the challenges it presents."

The survey would not only become a useful indicator of Kupenda's impact but of where future assistance was needed most. It would also become apparent that Kupenda needed to increase its advocacy efforts in the communities it served. Some suggestions for this included providing Leonard and his team with viable transportation for child outreach, creating mobile clinics to visit people in their homes, establishing more sign language workshops, and establishing vocational programs. At present, children who graduated were given one additional year of sponsorship to help pay for tools for their vocation.

When one student named Shehe Karisa finished school, he received some tools for carpentry. While gaining experience, he was even able to teach his employer some sign language. Eventually he began helping with furniture repair and working for a construction company that assisted with roofing at the Gede School.

On the heels of Alanna's visit, another couple from the United States would visit Kenya to conduct a survey of a handful of pastors in the area to determine their beliefs about disability and their understanding of the Bible. It would be discovered that many of the pastors lacked formal training in biblical literature. This would be one more indicator that pastor workshops hosted by the organization were still very much needed.

Unfortunately, as Kupenda planned ahead for its future, a current disruption in Kenya was causing things to come to a grinding halt.

CHAPTER 24

SCAPEGOATS

Evil starts like the prick of a needle and spreads like a tree.—African Proverb

Kenya, 2009

Cindy received news that Kenyan teachers were on strike. This was not an altogether uncommon experience, but it was one that was still problematic. This time they were protesting their low salaries nationwide. The government-run schools that Kupenda supported were now shut down until the staff returned. This included schools in the Malindi District, whose boundary lines were recently changed by the creation of a new Margarini District that included the school in Marafa. Meanwhile, children were returned to their homes, many of which were not equipped to meet their needs for nutrition and care.

Fortunately, the strike had resolved by the time Andy and his wife, Kate, arrived with a volunteer group in June. One of the volunteers, named Fran, was a special-needs teacher and was able to instruct other teachers on how to write individual education plans for each student. After doing practical exercises and discussing their experiences, Fran was touched when two mainstream teachers attending the workshop chose to take the courses necessary to become special-education teachers.

During the rest of her stay, the volunteers illustrated sensory teaching techniques for the other teachers, including having the children dance the macarena and to the song "YMCA." At one point, the children even formed a playful conga line. Additionally, they left textbooks about special education and disabilities in the Kupenda office, which doubled as a resource center. Before its creation, many of the teachers needed to travel more than eight hours to Nairobi to get materials that might be outdated by as many as twenty years.

Yet another source of encouragement was the development of a disability guidebook that Cindy and other collaborators worked to publish. The guide outlined symptoms, causes, and treatment for various disabilities in an easy-to-understand summary, which was distributed in English and Swahili.

For one boy named Erick, disability was a life-and-death matter. While the volunteers were visiting Kenya, Erick's father took him to the Kupenda office in a desperate plea for help. His son was born with albinism, which resulted in a severe case of skin cancer with tumors protruding from his face. As Cindy broadcast the need back at home, a middle school teacher named Rob Irias rose to the challenge. Asking children at his school to help, he organized a bike-a-thon. The students rode their bikes around a predetermined loop as sponsors paid them per lap. The bike-a-thon team raised thousands of dollars and was able to fund Erick's medical care. The treatment Erick received helped spare his life. For the next few years, he rededicated himself to his studies, aspiring to be a lawyer. Eventually, however, the disease took hold of his body and ultimately his life. Through a handful of kids an ocean away, however, he was given hope and a few more years with the ones he loved.

On the heels of this endeavor came another crisis. The head teacher at the Gede Special School, Madam Karo, noticed unusual behavior from a ten-year-old deaf student, referred to by the pseudonym Imara. She noticed that Imara had been resisting going home and had even run away from her aunt when she visited her at school. Concerned, Madam Karo brought up the issue before a committee. She also asked a family member to investigate if there were any problems at home.

When Imara later showed up to school with blood in her underwear, Madam Karo took action and had the girl taken to a clinic. When it was determined that she had been sexually assaulted, Madam Karo called the authorities to come to the school. Surrounded by unwanted attention, Imara was petrified by the police's questions. As a result, one policewoman took Imara aside to talk privately, along with one of her friends in a wheelchair who could interpret for her. There Imara allegedly reported that the abuse took place at home by her cousin. Later when she was taken to the police station, she was reported to have pointed out her perpetrator, who was jailed. Neighbors allegedly also confirmed the identity of the perpetrator, citing past incidents of sexual abuse between the girl and her relatives. Soon afterward, however, the boy was released due to Section 143 of the Kenya penal code, which stated "A male person under the age of twelve (12) years is presumed to be incapable of having carnal knowledge." Since it was often difficult to prove one's birth date in Kenya if he or she had been born at home, the boy previously thought by some to be thirteen years old was claiming to be younger than age twelve.

A short while later a new accusation surfaced. The mother of another child arrived at the school, stating that she had spoken to Imara at the police station. She claimed Imara told her the rape had been committed by two deaf boys at the school. The accused were the same two boys who were punished for stealing mangoes the day before. For Madam Karo and others involved, this was confusing on many levels. For one thing, the mother was not fluent in Kenyan sign language, and there was supposedly no interpreter at the police station. Furthermore, others described the mother as having a personal grudge against the head teacher ever since her husband was not reelected chair of the Gede Special School.

Complicating matters further was the religious tension between all parties. Imara's family was Muslim and supposedly did not want the shame of the situation brought on their family or religious community. As threats were made to Madam Karo, the teacher's union stepped in to defend her. Meanwhile, as the two accused boys were jailed without an interpreter, they staunchly defended their innocence by partaking in a hunger strike. As a result, Kupenda hired a lawyer to represent them and provided an interpreter.

As the whole situation was brought to trial, witnesses reported that it was clear that the court interpreter was not fluent in Kenyan sign language. Additionally, Imara's friend in the wheelchair who had witnessed Imara's initial police report had passed away and was no longer able to testify, sparking rumors that the Muslim community had cursed her. Nevertheless, there were many accounts from people in the courtroom citing evidence in favor of the boys' innocence, but when the verdict was finally declared, the boys were found guilty. Also striking was their sentence. Section 140 of the Penal Code stated that a person accused of rape may be liable with imprisonment and hard labor for life, along with the possibility of corporal punishment. However, in this case, the judge declared the boys guilty and then allowed them off with a simple probation. Within minutes, there were whispers of a bribe—one supposedly meant to send a message from the Muslim community without actually sending two innocent boys to jail. In response to the entire ordeal, members of the Kupenda board began to draft sexual abuse prevention and defense curriculum to be taught to staff and students—something not even commonly found among disability communities in the Western world.

Despite the setback, Cindy and Leonard tried to remain focused on small measures of progress. This was evident in the lives of one of their students, Oliver, when his mother arrived at the school after previously abandoning her son. Years ago, Oliver developed cerebral palsy after contracting cerebral malaria at five months old. He was unable to sit up on his own or lift his head. One night when he continued to cry, his mother could not contain her frustration any longer and told her son, "I wish you could die so that your grandmother and I could rest."

She even visited a woman in the community asking for advice. She was informed that the best option was "to eliminate that useless creature, which has no future" through starvation or poisoning.

Upon hearing this, the grandmother became furious with her daughter for even considering such an option. Overwhelmed by trying to support the child's needs amid a growing famine in the area, the mother took her younger child and left town, leaving Oliver with his grandmother for good.

It was not until a relative in Malindi told Oliver's grandmother about assistance for children with disabilities in Gede that she began to hope. Bringing the boy to the assessment center, she learned that the special school at Gede was full. Instead, Oliver was referred to a school in Marafa, a town that the grandmother felt was much too far away. As a result, the assessment officer referred Oliver to Kupenda. When the grandmother came to Leonard's office to request support, he searched until he found a small home nearby that agreed to accept the child.

After Oliver was in the school for a year, his mother resurfaced with the hope that her child had died and she might return home. With great efforts of persuasion, the grandmother finally convinced the mother to visit Oliver, who was very much still alive. When she arrived at the school, she was unable to tell which child was hers. None of the children before her looked like the boy she had left behind.

When the grandmother directed her to her son, she stated, "My daughter, this is Oliver, your son you left more than a year ago."

Before her, Oliver straightened out his hand and gave her a huge smile. Overcome, she wept as she lifted her son out of his wheelchair. The child she once hid was now a source of hope. With three meals a day, good medical care, and therapeutic exercises, Oliver was thriving. Embracing them both, the grandmother also wept.

In the coming months, both women continued to visit the child. Transformed by the aid they received, they even took it upon themselves to share their experiences with other mothers in hopes of preventing the mistreatment and neglect of other children with disabilities.

Just like with Oliver's mother, Leonard also found it important to educate other parents about their ownership of their children's health. Just like in the United States, it was sadly not unheard of for parents to use their child's disability as an income generator in order to receive assistance. A child missing one finger was brought to Kupenda's attention, despite the fact that the child was able to function normally in a mainstream classroom. Thankfully, the organization helped safeguard against such attempts for money by visiting homes and observing the quality of life of families firsthand, as well as offering medical evaluations for the children. Leonard also asked parents to take ownership of their child by paying a percentage of school fees whenever possible.

Unfortunately, some parents could not even afford toiletries. It was not uncommon to find that a child was kept out of school simply because he or she could not afford such items as a toothbrush, let alone a school uniform. Other children had no money for transportation. When they did not arrive at school, Leonard or another staff member would check on them in their homes, sometimes finding them sitting unattended outside with the livestock.

Concerned about children left in such neglect, Leonard pursued local orphanages who might look after the children during school breaks, to no avail. While he did not want to encourage parents of children with disabilities to abandon their children so that Kupenda would care for them, he hoped to find some sort of solution. Perhaps the housemothers could be paid to stay at the school over breaks. But this would remain a dream until the organization could acquire the necessary funds to pull it off.

Meanwhile, Cindy arrived in Kenya with her own hope struggling to surface. She was still recovering from her broken engagement over Christmas as a result of personal obstacles the two were facing. On the week she was to have been married, she sat in Leonard's office, trying to operate beyond her grief. It was during this time that she encountered a midwife who came to the office, lamenting the condition of a baby who had recently been born with a disability. As the woman explained, the infant's mother was so distraught over what she might have done for her child to be born with a disability that she refused to venture outside of her home. After listening to her story, Leonard encouraged the midwife to go back to the mother and urge her to meet with him. In just a couple of days, the midwife managed to return, this time with the parents and baby in tow.

As introductions were made, Cindy observed that the three week old infant named Joyce had bands tied around one of her wrists, traditionally believed to ward off evil spirits. As she examined the baby more closely, she also noticed that part of the girl's left arm was missing, just like her own. Lifting the baby in her arms, she cuddled the newborn with a palpable empathy.

Beside her, Leonard and Reverend Mangi openly discussed Cindy's similar condition and what she had been able to achieve. The parents were astonished that such a disability could even happen to a mzungu, or white person. Furthermore, the fact that Cindy could complete simple tasks like tying her hair back was astonishing, let alone that she was able to drive or play the guitar. They continued to listen to the way God had used Cindy's arm condition to influence her heart to help hundreds of others and their concerns began to slowly diminish. In its place, the weaknesses and strengths of Cindy's life fit together into a body of evidence that represented a life-altering hope.

The mother stated, "Now I know that my daughter will accomplish what other children do, and one day maybe she can even bless others the way Kupenda does."

Her heart buoyed, Cindy realized that if all she ever did for Kupenda was help this one child, it would all be worthwhile. She reflected on God's choice to use her disability to comfort others. Just as he had not forgotten Joyce, he would not forget her in her sorrow. It was a confirmation of her call, bringing new meaning to Ephesians 2:10, which stated, "For we are God's handiwork created in Christ Jesus to do good works, which God prepared in advance for us to do."

CHAPTER 25

REUNION

He will wipe every tear from their eyes. There will be no more death or mourning or crying or pain, for the old order of things has passed away.—Revelation 21:4

Kenya, 2010

A short while after her return to the United States, Cindy admitted that she could no longer work a full-time job as well as manage a rapidly growing non-profit for free. Spearheading these efforts, the board chairperson campaigned to get Cindy into a fully funded position. After a lengthy reorganization process, Cindy officially took a paid position as executive director, spending months catching up on a backlog of details so the organization's growth could continue once again.

Meanwhile, another form of progress was also taking place in Kenya. The country drafted a new constitution that protected the rights of people with disabilities, including voting rights, adequate political representation, proper access to alternative forms of communication, access to education, and the right to participate in all levels of public service.

At the same time, Andy and his wife, Kate, returned to Kenya with a volunteer group. For the first time, the volunteers were able to take twenty-two children, teachers, and parents to surrounding areas of their community that were usually reserved for tourists. For many of the students

Kupenda supported, this was also the first time they had experienced the ocean, despite living only five miles away.

Unfortunately, along with these steps forward came another step back. Cindy learned that the Kenyan government was trying to separate the children at the main school in Gede, attempting to remove forty-eight of the seventy-two deaf children at the Gede Special School to a new boarding facility in Kakuyuni. This was despite the fact that there were more than sixty children identified who had hearing impairments in the district who were still not enrolled in any school. As a result, Leonard had to battle with the District Education Office using the National Special Needs Education Policy Framework, a document written by the Kenyan Ministry of Education, as his weapon to fight for the children to stay together in one community. As he explained, the children depended on one another. The government only provided four housemothers to care for more than 130 children, thirty of whom were in wheelchairs. The deaf children helped to push the mobility-challenged students in their wheelchairs, while the students in the wheelchairs often translated sign language to others. They depended on one another like two different ends of the same lever, alternately lifting one another up when needed. The community at the school was one that used the gifts of every student to create a thriving whole. Consequently, Kuhenza made a commitment to watch over the school to ensure the children remained with one another.

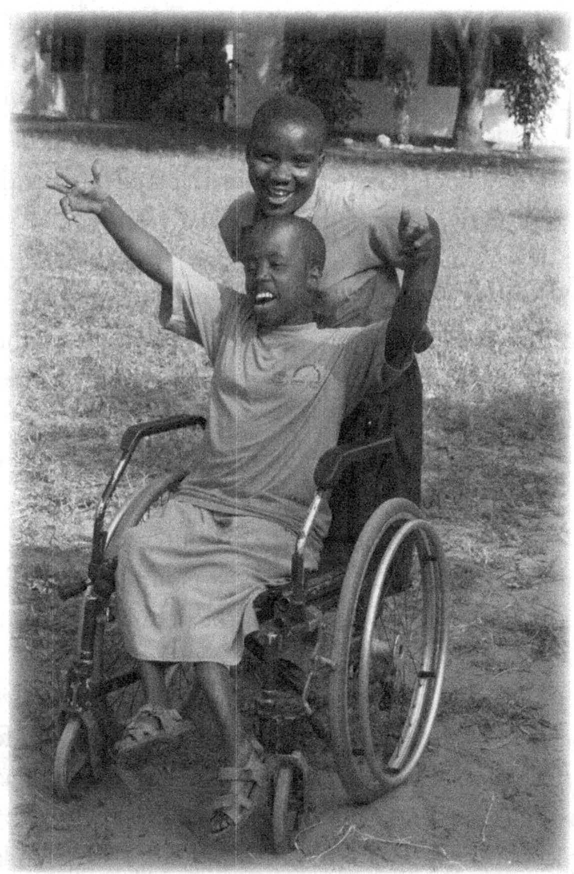

A student who is deaf helping another student with mobility at the Gede Special School in 2007.

After Leonard met with the district education officer in person, more details came to light about the government worker's motivations for moving the children. The worker was accused of a high level of insubordination for trying to move the children for personal gain. It also became apparent that certain individuals at the Gede Special School stood to benefit by being offered promotions if the children were moved. After multiple discussions, the worker was given a warning, and the district education officer agreed to let the children stay where they were.

As Leonard concluded, "These children are not animals that you just send to graze in other pastures when you feel like it."

Cindy and Leonard hoped to continue keeping a close eye on the almost six hundred children in nineteen schools the organization supported. Of that number, about one hundred sixty children needed sponsorship fees, including 90 percent of the special-needs students at the Gede Special School. The progress of the students continued to be encouraging, however. There had even been a 57 percent increase in the number of children attending high school.

Although proud of this success, Cindy still worried about estimates of need from the assessment center in the district—four hundred to five hundred children who had yet to be assisted due to limited staff and resources, and five hundred or more children who had not even been located yet. Those numbers did not include the children in the new Margarini District where the Marafa School was located.

Cindy was often tempted to become discouraged, and she reflected on a quote by Mother Teresa, which stated, "We ourselves feel that what we are doing is just a drop in the ocean. But the ocean would be less because of that missing drop."

It was not until 2012 that the special unit Kupenda supported in Marafa became elevated to a special school of its own, boasting room for sixty-two children and six teachers. Part of this success was due to an additional dormitory funded by South Mountain Community Church in Utah. The new sleeping quarters alleviated congestion in the other dormitory where children moved beds into shower stalls. Due to chronic water shortages in the area, the showers were not able to be used. Helping with this situation, Mosaic Christian Church in Maryland held an Advent Conspiracy, asking its congregation to forego one gift at Christmas to support a water project for Kupenda. At the end of the holiday season, the church raised the funds needed to help.

Since African water projects were notorious for going wrong, Kupenda researched its options and collaborated with other organizations to look into the water tables in the area. The most popular solution of drilling a well would, in this case, end up depleting the water source for multiple surrounding villages. Instead, Kupenda constructed a rain catchment system and supplemented this water supply with the transportation of additional water during the dry seasons. Now when Cindy visited the school, the children's freshly laundered clothes were hung on a line, and they gleefully ran to fill their mugs with water.

Kenya, 2011

As another year progressed, Cindy continued to visit Kenya despite its latest military conflict. After decades of war in Somalia, which caused hundreds of thousands of refugees to flee to Kenya, a Somali militant group called al-Shabab was accused of kidnapping foreign aid workers and causing acts of violence that continued to spread to the capital and down the coast. In response, the Kenyan government was reported to have sent troops into Somalia. Unfortunately, the effects on the tourism industry and the safety of volunteers and aid workers were still creating damage. As a result, the already impoverished region was even more strapped for resources and assistance than ever.

Focusing on one piece of the puzzle at a time, Cindy made a conscious effort to keep in touch with Joyce, the child she met while healing from her broken engagement. Visiting Joyce's home, she embraced the shy girl and the arm that would most likely categorize her as different all of her life. As the extended family gathered, they asked Cindy to demonstrate more of her abilities.

Cindy took to the local customs, showing the family how she too was able to carry a water jerrycan on her head or grind corn. In an environment where work equals survival, these were keys to an independent and sustainable life. Cindy continued to challenge the family to view their daughter not as a burden but as a source of boundless possibility.

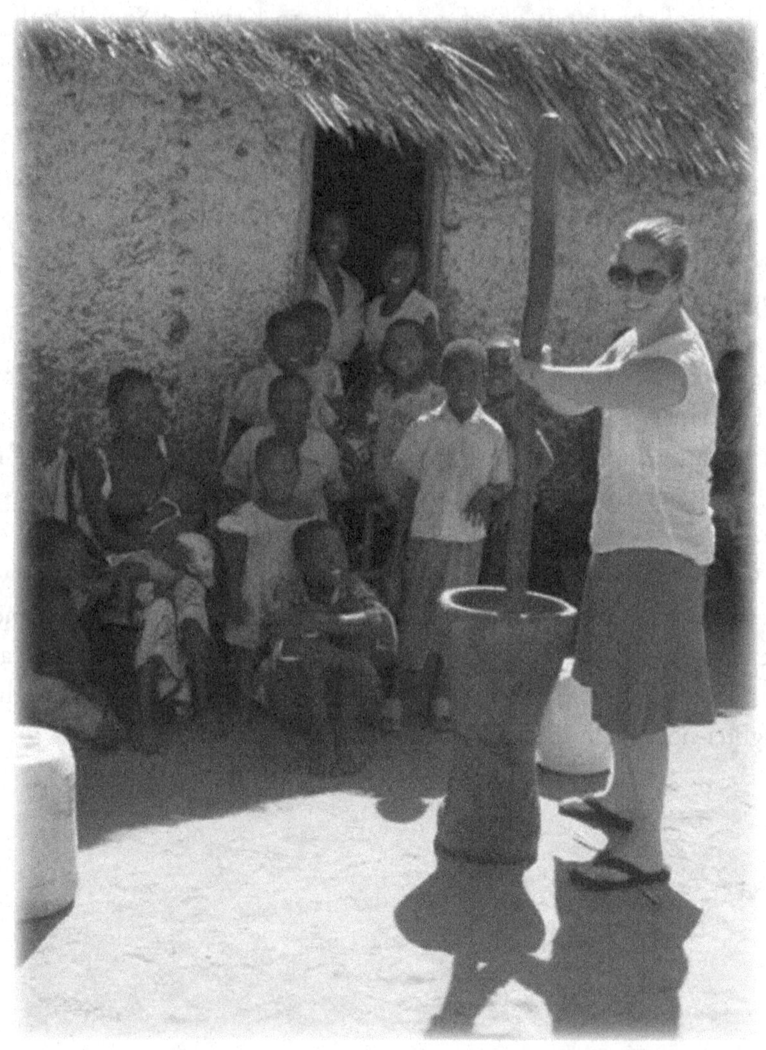

Cindy demonstrating her ability to grind corn with one arm in front of Joyce's family in 2010.

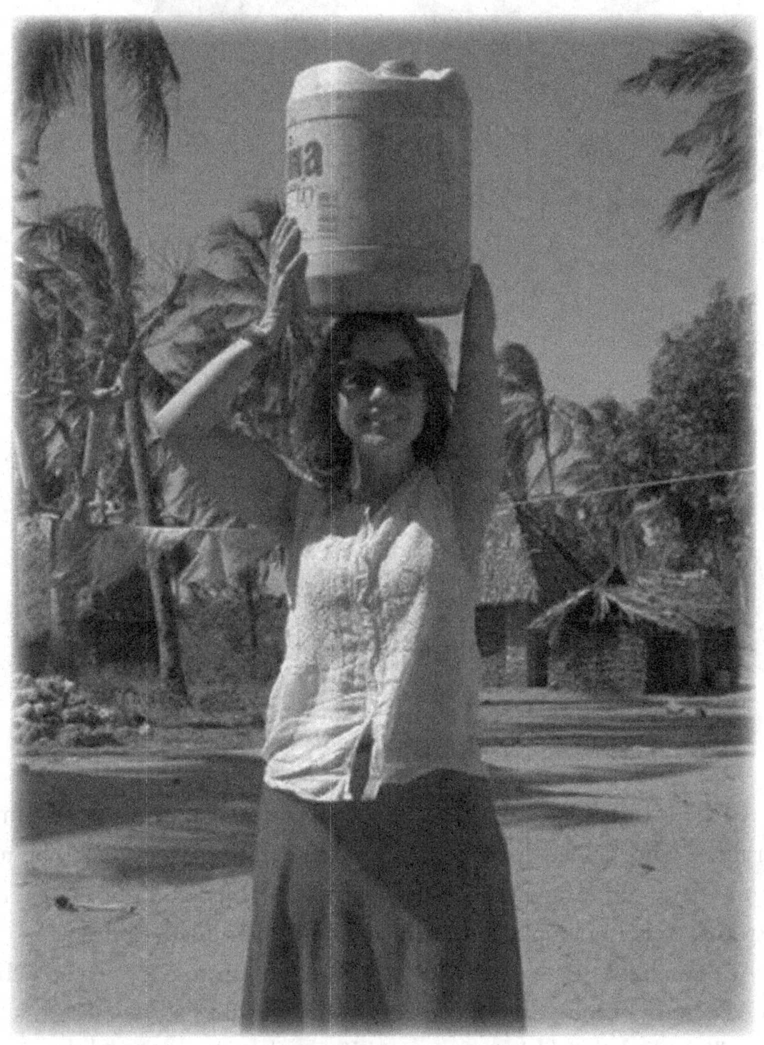

Cindy demonstrating how to carry water with one arm in front of Joyce's family in 2010.

Cindy with Joyce in 2012.

At the office, Cindy visited Leonard's new assistant director named Maryline, who helped him with his overwhelming workload. She also saw the new sign language book a volunteer named Julia Spruance had illustrated to help parents communicate with their deaf children.

At the school, she visited with other students and marveled at a child named Jeremy. One year ago Jeremy was only able to scoot across the floor. With the help of his sponsor and Kupenda's occupational therapists, including longtime employee Elizabeth Mtie, he was able to progress to the point of using a walker. While at the school, Jeremy was frequently darting around the buildings with his mobility aid, leaving tracks like a cursive signature behind him. In just a short while, he successfully took his first steps without a walker. With his newfound freedom, he loved to run up to volunteers, seemingly coming out of nowhere and affectionately clinging to them. His huge smile never left his face as he ran among the other children, an act that never ceased to grow old for him as he remained constantly in motion.

Cindy saw this same message of hope applied to the life of Kupenda's first sponsored child, Charo Shida. The five-year-old boy she had met while completing her wildlife research more than a decade ago had grown in numerous ways. He had advanced in his knowledge of sign language and made many new friends. His life was like a periodic table that was always gathering new rows. Instead of metal and gas, he had language and community—elements that offered a new complexity of meaning to his life that he could not have known otherwise. In fact, his progress also spurred his mother, who had originally abandoned him for his disability, to reemerge in his life. Sadly, it turned out it would not be for long as she died a short while later.

Now Leonard was sending word that Charo Shida himself had reached the end of his life much too soon, passing away after multiple epileptic seizures. Charo was particularly special to Cindy because he was the first Kupenda-sponsored child and she had personally paid for his school fees. Out of consideration, Charo's grandparents, who had acted as his guardians for most of his life, decided to postpone the funeral until Cindy arrived with a volunteer team the following week. It was important to them that they shared in their grief together.

Cindy with Charo Shida in 2006.

At the funeral, among the wailing and cultural displays of grief, she delivered a eulogy she practiced in Swahili. Looking out at the audience, she saw an entire community celebrating the life of a child who might have once been entirely ignored. She also saw her dad in attendance, marking the first time he made the trek to Kenya to witness and celebrate the work being done. As with Cindy and many of the children, the Lord chose to bring gifts and healing through people whose own communities scorned or rejected them—just like his own son.

As the ceremony continued, Charo Shida's grandparents placed a handful of dirt on the coffin and reflected on how their child loved helping others. They watched as their boy, along with his aspirations of becoming a doctor, was placed beneath a layer of soil.

Next in succession, Madam Karo placed a handful of dirt on the coffin. She remembered the boy's big smile, how he was always the first person to run and greet visitors at the school gates, offering to carry their bags. She watched as the student, along with his eagerness to assist, was placed beneath another layer of soil.

Cindy in turn also spread dirt over the coffin, reflecting on how Charo Shida's name, which meant "journey of problems," marked the hard yet beautiful road to Kupenda's beginning.

Although Charo's journey on Earth had ended, the journey he began for Kupenda was not yet complete. He left a legacy of hundreds of children who would benefit from the love shown to children with disabilities. She watched as the Kupenda-sponsored child's coffin became covered and the earth stilled, Charo Shida never knowing the impact he made on so many.

Although he had been buried, he was not to be forgotten. Cindy clung to the hope that through all of the efforts and challenges placed in Kupenda's path, that she would once again see the child that helped create her life's greatest work and deepest meaning. The Charo Shida she saw then would be the first person to greet her, but this time fully restored.

While the earth may have been still, eternity had stirred.

AFTERWORD

2012–Present

Reading through the stories Lauren so eloquently captured brings back the emotions and memories of the joys and sorrows of Kupenda's development as if I was reliving them. It seems like yesterday and yet so long ago at the same time. The idea to finally write this book was realized when I was heartbroken about the end of my engagement in 2009. It seemed like the right time to revisit how God has used brokenness for his purposes. I knew I didn't have the time or talent to do something like this and am so grateful that Lauren felt this was her calling. In spite of the difficult life circumstances encountered through the writing process and the abundance of information gathered, Lauren has wonderfully woven the many people and stories that have resulted in Kupenda's existence. She even left her job as she continued her role as board chair, to write this book. In addition to all that Lauren has done for Kupenda as an organization, she has been an amazing friend and encourager to me. She flew to my house after my engagement ended and helped me continue on with the work when funding and time made it seem impossible to continue.

We often speak of our relationship as similar to Aaron and Moses when Israel was fighting the Amalekites. When Moses' hands were up, the Israelites were winning and when down, they would lose. Therefore Aaron (and Hur) held up his hands when he did not have the strength to do it alone. I am grateful to Lauren for providing strength when mine seemed nonexistent. I think holding up the weak arms is a more important job than being the more visibly powerful one. I hope that, through this book, you've seen how God uses brokenness and weakness for good and that he never calls us to do his work alone even if we feel isolated at times.

A friend once described Kupenda as a great work God invited us to be part of. God rarely gives me much advanced notice about what is next no matter how hard I try to predict it. Therefore, between writing this epilogue and publishing, even more is bound to happen. I'm confident of the changes on the horizon because in just the two years since Charo's funeral, there have been new initiatives, stories of children saved from the brink, heartbreaks, and amazing joy.

Charo's death effected Leonard and me deeply, but our grief motivated us to make the idea of a Kupenda-created and run school a reality. We are only in the proposal stages of our own school for children with disabilities, but we have hope that one day the dream will be realized and that it will serve as a model school for others to replicate. We envision the first stages of development being a supplement to existing schools. We will start with serving those who are hard of hearing and children with cerebral palsy who need communication assistance, as well as providing autism support services and a place for adults with disabilities who are unable to live independently. We have already started to serve children who are hard of hearing through hard-of-hearing workshops.

In January 2012 an American volunteer who is hard of hearing shared his incredible musical talent with those like him. The children who saw him perform believe they can do more than they ever imagined. Now that they know what is possible, we need to provide the needed services to support them in their new vision of their futures.

We also plan to have the school serve children with severe cerebral palsy, focusing on alternative communication. So many of the children we've met have amazing minds trapped inside broken bodies, unable to share their thoughts with the world and no one with the time or expertise to make this possible. Autism cases are increasing at an alarming rate in Kenya, and we need to provide specialized help for these children. In January 2013, three volunteers specializing in autism worked with children who have autism in Kenya and saw dramatic results in days. One child with autism was found chained to his house and, after working with these volunteers, was laughing and smiling. Kupenda has also recently partnered with a research organization to lead a coastal-wide autism support network.

Finally, children with dependent disabilities are getting too old for the schools they are in, and their families are not equipped to assist them.

Currently there are no facilities for dependent adults in the area, and we would like to provide this for them. The school vision includes a teaching staff of Kenyans and Westerners so they can learn from each other, providing the most effective support for these kids. A school created and run by Kupenda is daunting, but all of what we've done so far has started with an idea that seemed overwhelming at first. We know this "journey of problems" started with Charo Shida, but it will not end with his death. We are determined that his death will only be another sorrowfully joyous beginning. Therefore, the school will be named after him.

In June 2012, I was tired and sad and thought about giving it all up. I've heard from many people who work in non-profit work or ministry that multiple moments of this kind of despair is common. Both Leonard and I were experiencing our own personal heartbreaks, funding was uncertain, and I was (and still am) the only one working full time in the United States. All of it just made me feel abandoned, alone, and hopeless. Many of my spiritual mentors and friends thought maybe the call had been fulfilled (after twelve years), and it was time to move on to something else. I investigated alternative employment yet still felt like I should go to the Beyond Suffering Class and conference offered by Joni and Friends (started by Joni Eareckson Tada). Its intent is for students to have a better understanding of disability within a Christian context. It was being offered just two miles down the road from me so it was hard to ignore. Part of me thought maybe it would be my last act as Kupenda director. The class and conference were great for making new connections that have resulted in enormous financial and spiritual benefits. I now meet weekly with a small group of women who were in my class who are ten to fifteen years older than me, giving them the role of older sisters in my life. Perhaps a better description would be that they are like supportive angels providing encouragement beyond what I could have hoped. They have also connected Kupenda to bigger donors than we've ever had. We just received our first official larger-scale grant and have another on its way. In January 2013, two skilled American volunteers and I taught a modified version of the Beyond Suffering Course in Kenya to equip leaders to teach it in their communities. Members of the class have already started an autism support group for parents and are educating their churches and communities about the value of people with disabilities. It is so exciting to see Kupenda's impact increase throughout the local community. Again, out of my despair, God provided much more than I could have ever imagined.

Although all of what I mentioned has been amazing, the most impactful event in the last two years was at the end of the June 2012 class and conference. I'm not a very emotion-filled worshiper, so what happened was very surprising to me. The very last song we sang was "It Is Well with My Soul," and it was during the last verse that something powerful occurred. The words of the last verse are as follows:

> "And Lord, haste the day when my faith shall be sight,
> The clouds be rolled back as a scroll;
> The trump shall resound, and the Lord shall descend,
> Even so, it is well with my soul."

During this verse I just couldn't sing anymore or open my eyes. As tears were streaming down my face, I saw the children we serve in Kenya at the gates of heaven. Those who were in wheelchairs were getting up and walking in, and the deaf were singing, with Charo Shida leading the way. God was answering my cries of loneliness and discouragement with a reminder of what our work in Kenya is all about. He didn't tell me how the details would work out or if my heart would heal the way I desired, but he reminded me of why we do what we do. Even with the challenges and heartbreak, he is involved, and it continues to be the calling he has placed on me even when I am ready to quit. He not only reaffirms my calling, he continues to call others to join him in serving these beautiful children.

It seems that as the impact of Kupenda grows, so do the trials. I've started to believe that the bigger the obstacle, the more amazing the work God has in store. Often with this journey, just when everything seems impossible, God shows himself in ways I could never expect. Looking back on all the ways God has provided, I have hope that he will again come through in spite of how difficult things might seem. Lauren and I often discussed what the afterword of this book would be like, and we fantasized about a "happy ending"—but that's not real life. We didn't anticipate the struggles we've both encountered over the last few years, nor did we anticipate the joy. For example, Lauren just gave birth to a baby boy. He is truly a miracle we had almost given up hope as Lauren suffered through the pain of multiple miscarriages and a failed adoption during the writing of this book. It gives me hope that miracles still and will happen for the organization and for those of us who are still suffering from loss and heartbreak. Although there are still hard things, I have confidence that God is in control even if the intended beauty is painful at first.

As much as I plan and organize, I am reminded often that Kupenda wasn't my idea, and God is not yet finished with Kupenda or with me. This is not the end of the story.

Cynthia Bauer
Founder and Executive Director,
Kupenda for the Children

ABOUT THE AUTHOR

Lauren Boswell Blair is an author and experienced policy writer for multiple government agencies and contractors. She is also the acting chairperson for the non-profit Kupenda for the Children. A graduate of the University of Mary Washington, she lives in Baltimore, Maryland, with her husband, Patrick; son, Grayson; and Goldendoodle, Macy.

REFERENCES

"Act 14 of 2003—Persons with Disabilities," accessed March 29, 2013, http://dredf.org/international/Kenya2.pdf.

"African Proverbs, Sayings and Stories," accessed April 25, 2013, http://www.afriprov.org/index.php/african-proverb-of-the-month/23-1998proverbs/26-july-1998.html.

"Afritorial: The Best 72+ African Wise Proverbs and Inspiring Quotes," accessed April 9, 2013, http://afritorial.com/the-best-72-african-wise-proverbs/.

Ahlers, Alanna. "Exposing the Attitudes and Perceptions toward the Disabled Population in Malindi, Kenya: Assessment of the Impact of Kupenda for the Children," Kupenda research paper, 2009.

"American College of Surgeons," accessed April 5, 2013, http://www.operationgivingback.facs.org/content3180.html.

"American Society for Surgery of the Hand," accessed March 29, 2013, http://www.assh.org/Public/HandConditions/Pages/CongenitalHandDifferences.aspx.

Andrew Bauer (Kupenda board member), interview with the author, June 19, 2009.

Anthony Jomo Kenyatta (former Kupenda-sponsored child), interview with the author, January 20, 2010.

Anthony Maranto (Kupenda board member), interview with the author, September 20, 2009.

"A Policy Framework for Education," accessed March 29, 2013, http://fieldmarshamfoundation.org/wp-content/uploads/tumblr/References/Policy%20Framework%20For%20Education%20Paper%20Kenya%20School%20Libraries.pdf.

Bauer, Cynthia Rose. "Impact of Commercial and Subsistence Practices on the Arabuko Sokoke Forest in Coastal Kenya, Using an Endemic Mammal as an Indicator Species." Thesis, Eastern Kentucky University, 2001.

Bauer, Dick. March 22, 1974. "Grandpa Letter." Private collection.

Bauer, Sandra. "Gerard Wilbur Is Awarded WWII Silver Star 63 Years After Discharge." *The Ellsworth American*, September 11, 2008.

Bauer, Sandra. April 26, 2009. "Cindy's Birth." Private collection.

Beatrice Plowman, interview with the author, April 9, 2009.

Benyawa, Linah. 2013. "A Win for Disabled, the Youth." *Standard Digital News—Kenya*, Accessed March 20, accessed March 21, 2013. http://www.standardmedia.co.ke/?articleID=2000079709&story_title=A-win-for-disabled% 2C-the-youth.

"Bethany Kids," accessed March 29, 2013, http://www.bethanykids.org/.

Boop, Emily. "Disability Rights in Kenya," Kupenda pamphlet, 2010.

Brian Buell (Kupenda board member), interview with the author, June 18, 2009.

Brianna Riddell (Kupenda volunteer), interview with the author, June 18, 2009.

Charo Shida family (family of former Kupenda-sponsored child), interview with the author, translated by Maryline Faida, January 13, 2012.

"The Children's Act: 2001," accessed March 29, 2013, http://sgdatabase.unwomen.org/uploads/Children%20Act%20-%202001.pdf.

Claiborne, Laura and Melissa Kane. "Disabilities In Kenya: Disability Is Not Inability," Kupenda booklet, 2008.

"The Constitution of Kenya, 1969," accessed March 29, 2013, http://www.marsgroupkenya.org/Reports/LawsandConventions/Constitution_of_Kenya.pdf.

"The Constitution of Kenya, 2010," accessed March 29, 2013, http://www.kenyaembassy.com/pdfs/The%20Constitution%20of%20Kenya.pdf.

Cynthia Bauer (Kupenda Founder and Executive Director), interviews and discussions with the author, 2009–13.

Dick Bauer, interview with the author, June 17, 2009.

Dick Bransford (orthopedic surgeon), interview with the author, March 6, 2010.

Dick Wright (Pastor and Kupenda board member), interview with the author, July 18, 2009.

Eareckson Tada, Joni and Steve Bundy. *Beyond Suffering: A Christian View on Disability Ministry.* California: Joni and Friends, 2011.

Elizabeth Nthenya Mutie (Kupenda Occupational Therapist), interview with the author, January 18, 2010.

"Ethiopian Proverbs," accessed April 25, 2013, http://africanhistory.about.com/od/africanproverbs/p/EthiopianProverbs.htm.

Fran McConnell (Teacher, Kupenda volunteer), interview with the author, August 18, 2009.

Gabriel Mwnengo (Teacher, Gede Special School and Kuhenza Treasurer), interview with the author, January 19, 2010.

George Charo Mweri (Kupenda Parent of the Year), interview with the author, translated by Leonard Mbonani, January 18, 2012.

"Golden-Rumped Elephant Shrew," Wikipedia, accessed March 29, 2013, http://en.wikipedia.org/wiki/Golden-rumped_elephant_shrew.

"Google Maps: Lamu to Gede," accessed March 30, 2013, https://maps.google.com/maps?saddr=Lamu,+Kenya&daddr=Gede,+Kenya&hl=en&gl=us&panel=1&fb=1&dirflg=d&geocode=FYpe3f8dIRhwAimVFWWrPxkXGDE1KLo4zJHXfQ%3BFVUay_8doKtXAimXotuKtQA_GDHcUUtzYJ_-Jg&t=m&z=9.

"The Independent Kenya Travel Guide," accessed March 29, 2013, http://www.kenya-advisor.com/tribes-in-kenya.html.

"In Depth: Kenya's Post Election Crisis," accessed March 30, 2013, http://www.irinnews.org/In-depth/76116/68/Kenya-s-post-election-crisis.

Janet Mbonani, Dama, Kache, and Myevu, interview with the author, translated by Janet Mbonani and Leonard Mbonani, January 16, 2010.

Joyce Wanje and family (Kupenda-sponsored child and family), interview with the author, translated by Leonard Mbonani, January 22, 2010.

Julie Rowland, interview with the author, September 19, 2009.

Kate Bauer (Kupenda board member), interview with the author, August 11, 2009.

Ken Lawrence (Pastor), interview with the author, June 17, 2009.

Ken Turmet, interview with the author, March 21, 2010.

"Kenya Gazette Supplement No. 111 (Bills No. 51)," accessed March 29, 2013. http://www.kenyalaw.org/klr/fileadmin/pdfdownloads/bills/2012/BasicEducationBill2012.pdf.

"The Kenyan Military Intervention In Somalia," International Crisis Group, accessed March 30, 2013. http://www.crisisgroup.org/~/media/Files/africa/horn-of-africa/kenya/184%20-%20The%20Kenyan%20Military%20Intervention%20in%20Somalia.pdf.

"Kenya Society for the Mentally Handicapped," accessed March 30, 2013. http://www.ksmh.org/component/content/article/88/238-current-situation.

Koffa Edwin Abio (Kupenda Occupational Therapist), interview with the author, January 18, 2010.

Laura Claiborne (speech therapist), interview with the author, August 28, 2009.

Law Nolte, Dorothy. 1972. "Children Learn What They Live." Accessed March 27, 2013. http://www.empowermentresources.com/info2/childrenlearn-long_version.html.

"Legislation Of Interpol Member States On Sexual Offenses against Children: Kenya," accessed March 29, 2013. https://secure.interpol.int/Public/Children/SexualAbuse/NationalLaws/csaKenya.pdf.

Leonard Mbonani (Kuhenza Director), interview with the author, January 16, 2009.

Mabruk Salim (former Kupenda-sponsored child), interview with the author, translated by Chengo Kithi, January 20, 2010.

"Malindi District," Wikipedia, accessed March 29, 2013, http://en.wikipedia.org/wiki/Malindi_District.

"Malindi Weather Forecast," accessed March 29, 2013. http://www.weather-forecast.com/locations/Malindi/forecasts/latest.

Martha Karo (head teacher, Gede Special School), interview with the author, January 19, 2010.

Melissa Kane, interview with the author, September 16, 2009.

Moses Gona, interview with the author, translated by Leonard Mbonani, January 26, 2010.

"Mother Theresa Sayings," accessed April 6, 2013, http://www.mothertheresasayings.com/sayings.htm.

"Myoelectric Prosthetics," accessed March 29, 2013, http://www.myoelectricprosthetics.com/.
Nhu Lee, interview with the author, August 18, 2009.
Oliver Ngala and family (Kupenda-sponsored child and family), interview with the author, translated by Leonard Mbonani, January 21, 2010.
Patrick Blair and Adam Driscoll (Founders and Directors, Adventures for the Cure), interview with the author, August 24, 2009.
Patricia Prasada-Rao, interview with the author, October 17, 2009.
"Proverbatim," accessed April 25, 2013. http://www.proverbatim.com/ghanaian/ghanaian-misfortune-does-not-restrict-his.html.
"Proverbs," accessed April 19, 2013. http://goafrica.about.com/gi/o.htm?zi=1/XJ&zTi=1&sdn=goafrica&cdn=travel&tm=13&f=10&su=p284.13.342.ip_p531.60.342.ip_&tt=3&bt=0&bts=0&zu=http%3A//www.motherlandnigeria.com/proverbs.html.
"Proverbs from Africa," accessed April 25, 2013. http://poetryrose.beep.com/proverbs.htm.
Randy Wilbur (Pastor), interview with the author, June 19, 2009.
Rashid Athman (Kupenda-sponsored child), interview with the author, translated by Thelitha Wachu, January 20, 2010.
Rebecca Cross, interview with the author, June 20, 2009.
Robert Mangi (Reverend), interview with the author, June 18, 2010.
Sandra Bauer, interview with the author, June 18, 2009.
Scott Belfit, interview with the author, September 27, 2009.
Sirya (Assistant Chief), interview with the author, January 22, 2010.
Stejbach, Ken. 1991. "Bauer A Powerful Force." *The Hampton Union*, November 19.
Stewart, Julia. *African Proverbs and Wisdom*. New York: Kensington Publishing Corp., 1997.
Teede, Jan, and Fiona Teede. *The Zambezi: River of the Gods*. South Africa: Russel Friedman, 1991.
Teresia Zawadi and family (former Kupenda-sponsored child, Kuhenza intern and family), interview with the author, translated by Teresia Zawadi, January 20, 2010.
Thomas Katana (Kuhenza secretary), interview with the author, January 23, 2010.

"United Nations: Enable," accessed March 29, 2013. http://www.un.org/disabilities/default.asp?id=18.

Victoria Ndaa (Teacher, Gede Special School), interview with the author, January 18, 2010.

"Violence against Disabled Children," accessed March 29, 2013, http://www.unicef.org/videoaudio/PDFs/UNICEF_Violence_Against_Disabled_Children_Report_Distributed_Version.pdf.

Virginia Wilbur, interview with the author, June 19, 2009.

"Watamu Marine Association," accessed March 29, 2013. http://www.watamu.biz/watamu-attractions.php?cid=4.

Wilbur, Gerard. Undated correspondence to Cynthia Bauer. Private collection.

William Nganda (Guide, Arabuko Sokoke Forest), interview with the author, January 17, 2010.

"World Proverbs," accessed April 25, 2013. http://www.special-dictionary.com/proverbs/keywords/mosquito/.

Zeleza, Tiyambe. *Mijikenda*. New York: The Rosen Publishing Group, Inc., 1995.

Zurhura Masemo (Assessment Officer), interview with the author, January 19, 2010.

To make a donation to Kupenda for
the Children or to simply learn more,
please visit www.kupenda.org.

Endorsements

"From ancient times to the present there are those who have treated children with disabilities as being cursed by God. In this book, Lauren Blair not only challenges such benighted behavior but makes the case as to how such children can be viewed as gifts from God who can bless the rest of us."

—Tony Campolo,
Author/Speaker/Professor Emeritus of Sociology at Eastern University; Founder of the Evangelical Association for the Promotion of Education

"Lauren Blair … tells a story that will warm you heart—but not until it breaks it, deepens it, expands it, and fills it with love for beautiful African children you've not yet met."

—Brian D. McLaren,
Author/Speaker/Activist (brianmclaren.net)

"Kupenda reaches children with disabilities in Kenya—by any measure among the very least of the least. *An Unlikely Gift* tells their story and how Kupenda came to be. By the end of this book you will feel like part of the family."

—Ben Rhodes, PhD,
Christian Institute on Disability,
Joni & Friends International Disability Center

"*An Unlikely Gift* captures what I have experienced in Kenya during the last thirty years. Superstition, fear, and ignorance have isolated the disabled undoubtedly for centuries, but this is still true today. An intentional effort by organizations like Kupenda and the Almighty God seem to be slowly improving the situation in Kenya. Yet today there are forty to sixty other African countries with little, or no, care for their disabled."

—Dick Bransford, MD, FACS,
Co-Founder of Bethany Kids

"Kupenda has brought hope to the hopeless, love to those who never knew love, a home to the homeless, food to the hungry, light to the darkness, and happiness and laughter to the neglected."

—Martha Karo,
Head Teacher, Gede Special School, Kenya